THE REMINISCENCES OF
Rear Admiral Joseph C. Wylie, Jr. U.S. Navy (Retired)

INTERVIEWED BY
Paul Stillwell

U.S. Naval Institute • Annapolis, Maryland

Copyright © 2003

Preface

In the spring of 1985 I was in Newport, Rhode Island, to do some oral history work and was fortunate to be able to squeeze in two interviews with Admiral Wylie during my stay in the area. He was a delightful storyteller, and in retrospect I wish I had had more time available, because the interviews with him covered only the highlights of many of his tours of naval service and some not at all. For those topics that he did cover, he provided thoughtful, often entertaining discussion.

Admiral Wylie was a man devoted to the substance of his profession, whether it was on board a destroyer or in a billet ashore. And destroyers were his particular specialty. Though he began and ended his sea service on board cruisers, he spent the bulk of his time in destroyers: Reid, Bristol, Fletcher, Trever, Ault, and the staff of Commander Destroyer Flotilla One. He excelled in combat, particularly the hard fighting around Guadalcanal in late 1942. He also had the imagination and analytical ability to develop doctrine and operating procedures for destroyer combat information centers at a time in World War II when the benefits to be derived from radar were only gradually being appreciated in the fleet.

During his tours away from destroyers he frequently served on staffs and thus had an opportunity to observe top-flight leaders such as Harold Page Smith, Jimmy Thach, and Arleigh Burke. These added to the impressions he had gathered as a junior officer on board the heavy cruiser Augusta when his commanding officers were future admirals such as J. O. Richardson, Royal Ingersoll, and Chester Nimitz. Admiral Wylie's mind was able to focus on such mundane issues as consumption of beer on board ship and far, far broader issues such as why the nation has a Navy and what purposes that Navy should serve in concert with other services. He understood well the value of sea power and during the course of his career was often involved in the application of that power.

The transcript that follows is little altered from the way in which Admiral Wylie spoke the words into the tape recorder. I have introduced some footnotes to provide additional information for the benefit of readers. The volume includes two appendices in the form of letters that the admiral wrote to his grandson Peter. In these letters the grandfather went into greater detail on some topics than in the interviews themselves. I should also mention that Admiral Wylie did an oral history with Dr. Evelyn Cherpak of the Naval War College. A researcher would do well to read that transcript as well as this one. There is considerable overlap between the two versions, but each also contains material not to be found in the other.

Ms. Ann Hassinger of the Naval Institute's history division has made a significant contribution to the finished product through her diligence in the overall process of printing, proofreading, and overseeing the binding of the completed volume.

Paul Stillwell
Director, History Division
U.S. Naval Institute
February 2003

REAR ADMIRAL JOSEPH CALDWELL WYLIE, JR.
UNITED STATES NAVY (RETIRED)

Joseph Caldwell Wylie, Jr., was born in Newark, New Jersey, on 20 March 1911. He entered the U.S. Naval Academy, Annapolis, Maryland, on appointment from his native state in 1928. On 2 June 1932 he was graduated and commissioned ensign. Advancing progressively in rank, he subsequently attained that of rear admiral, to date from 1 December 1960.

Following graduation from the Naval Academy in 1932, he joined the USS Augusta (CA-31) and in May 1936 was assigned to the USS Reid (DD-369). He continued duty afloat from July 1938 until June 1939 in the USS Altair (AD-11), after which he served in the executive department at the Naval Academy. He reported on board the Bristol (DD-453) in July 1941 and was serving in that vessel when the United States entered World War II on 7 December 1941.

He was assigned in May 1942 as executive officer of the USS Fletcher (DD-445) and for "gallantry and intrepidity in action...[in that capacity] during night engagements with the enemy Japanese off Savo Island, Solomon Islands, on November 12 and 13 and November 30 and December 1, 1942..." he was awarded the Silver Star Medal. The citation further states in part: "Using discriminating judgment and quick resourcefulness, Lieutenant Commander Wylie directed the ship, gun and torpedo control of his vessel with outstanding success, inflicting heavy damage on two enemy cruisers and sinking a third..."

In January 1943 he assumed command of the USS Trever (DMS-16) and is entitled to the ribbon for the Navy Unit Commendation that was awarded that minesweeper for action in the Solomon Islands Campaign. Detached from command of the Trever in June 1943, he next served as Staff CIC Officer (Combat Information Center) on the staff of Commander Destroyer Force, Pacific. In March 1944 he reported as commanding officer of the USS Ault (DD-698) and during the period July to December 1945 served in the Office of the Commander in Chief, United States Fleet, with headquarters in the Navy Department, Washington, D.C. Attached to the Office of Naval Research as special project officer, he had duty in Jamestown, Rhode Island, and New York, until June 1948, when he reported as a student in strategy and tactics at the Naval War College, Newport, Rhode Island.

He was assigned to the staff of Commander Destroyer Flotilla One as staff operations officer from June 1949 until June 1950, after which he attended the advanced course at the Naval War College, Newport. In July 1953 he assumed command of the USS Arneb (AKA-56) and in July 1954 joined the staff of Commander Amphibious Group Two to serve as operations officer and later chief of staff and aide. In July 1955 he was ordered to duty in the Office of the Chief of Naval Operations, Navy Department, where he remained until October 1958, when he became commanding officer of the USS Macon (CA-132).

He served on the staff of the Supreme Allied Commander Atlantic from November 1959 until December 1960, when he assumed command of Cruiser Division Three (later redesignated Cruiser-Destroyer Flotilla Nine). He was Deputy Naval Inspector General, Navy Department, from November 1961 until August 1962, and then had duty with the Joint Strategic Survey Council, Joint Chiefs of Staff, Washington, D.C. For meritorious service in that assignment from 13 August 1962 to 1 June 1964, he was awarded the Joint Service Commendation Medal.

In July 1964 he reported as deputy chief of staff and deputy chief of staff for plans and operations to the Commander in Chief Atlantic Fleet and "for…outstanding service [in that capacity] during Operation Power Pack in the Dominican Republic crisis in April and May 1965…" he was awarded the Legion of Merit. The citation further states: "[He] provided invaluable assistance to the Commander in Chief United States Atlantic Fleet during a period when rapid, decisive planning and execution of joint military operations in the Dominican Republic were of the utmost importance to our national interests." In March 1966 he became Deputy Commander in Chief, U.S. Naval Forces Europe and chief of staff and aide to the Commander in Chief, U.S. Naval Forces Europe.

In October 1967 he was assigned as chief of staff and aide to the president of the Naval War College, Newport, Rhode Island, and in October 1968 became commander of the Naval Base, Newport, Rhode Island. His primary duty became additional duty in January 1969, when he reported as Commandant of the First Naval District, with headquarters in Boston, Massachusetts, with further additional duty as Commander Naval Base Newport and Commander Naval Base Boston. In January 1969 he was relieved of additional duty as Commander Naval Base Newport. "For meritorious conduct…as Commander of the First Naval District and Commander Naval Base, Boston from January 1969 to July 1972…" he was awarded a gold star in lieu of the second Legion of Merit. On 1 July 1972 he was transferred to the retired list of the U.S. Navy.

In addition to the Silver Star, the Legion of Merit and gold star, the Joint Service Commendation Medal, and the Navy Unit Commendation Ribbon, Rear Admiral Wylie was awarded the American Defense Service Medal; American Campaign Medal; European-African-Middle Eastern Campaign Medal; Asiatic-Pacific Campaign Medal; World War II Victory Medal; National Defense Service Medal with bronze star; and the Philippine Liberation Ribbon.

He was married to the former Harriette Bahney of Elizabeth, New Jersey. They had two children, Elizabeth G. Wylie and Peter Wylie. Admiral Wylie died 29 January 1993 at Portsmouth, Rhode Island.

Deed of Gift

The U.S. Naval Institute is hereby authorized to make available to individuals, libraries, and other repositories of its choosing the tapes and/or transcripts of two oral history interviews concerning the life and naval career of the late Rear Admiral Joseph C. Wylie, U.S. Navy (Retired). The interviews were recorded on 21 May 1985 and 22 May 1985, in collaboration with Paul Stillwell for the U.S. Naval Institute.

The undersigned does hereby release and assign to the U.S. Naval Institute the rights and title to these interviews, with the exception that the heirs of the interviewee retain the right to use the material for their own purposes, as they see fit. The copyright in both the oral and transcribed versions shall be the sole property of the U.S. Naval Institute. The tape recordings of the interviews are and will remain the property of the U.S. Naval Institute. The undersigned also stipulates that when any of the material in this oral history is used in published works—whether in printed format or electronic media—that any individual or individuals who have been criticized by Admiral Wylie in this work be identified in the published works only by title and not by name.

Signed and sealed this 18th day of January 2003.

Elizabeth G. Wylie
Elizabeth G. Wylie, for the estate of
Rear Admiral Joseph C. Wylie, U.S. Navy (Retired)

Interview Number 1 with Rear Admiral Joseph C. Wylie, Jr., U.S. Navy (Retired)

Place: Admiral Wylie's home, Portsmouth, Rhode Island

Date: Tuesday, 21 May 1985

Interviewer: Paul Stillwell

Paul Stillwell: To begin at the beginning, Admiral, would you tell where and when you were born and something about your parents and family background?

Admiral Wylie: Yes. Perfectly normal, no excitement, no notable parents. Born on the 20th of March, 1911 in Newark, New Jersey, and grew up mostly in Glen Ridge, which is part of the New York "bedroom." I went to high school in Newark, probably the only fellow I can think of that came to the Naval Academy from that area. I passed the entrance exams in February of 1928, and I heard about it in April. So I dropped out of high school and, until June, went down to Barnegat Bay, where Mother and Daddy had a house, and mostly sailed and horsed around until it was time to enter the Naval Academy. Now, what that translates is, I'm a high-school dropout that never went to college, because that was before the Naval Academy gave degrees.[*]

Paul Stillwell: What business was your father in?

Admiral Wylie: He was a manufacturer. He had come from South Carolina. He was a manufacturer, reasonably successful, not particularly notable. I was very fond of him, of course. A stable household, no broken homes, two younger sisters.

Since 1928 until I moved into this house in July of 1972, I was a government gypsy, living all over the country. I married after I came back from China in November of 1937. Two children, both of them now in service. Mrs. Wylie died in March of 1983. And what other vital statistics do you need?

Paul Stillwell: I'm interested in how you developed a desire to go to the Naval Academy.

---

[*] In 1933 a portion of that year's Naval Academy graduating class was not commissioned because of Depression-era economy measures. As a consequence, the academy began granting college degrees to its graduates that year, and some degrees were awarded retroactively for those who had graduated previously.

Admiral Wylie: I don't know. I've never been able to figure out why I went. I have a notion I watched my father commute on the Erie and Lackawanna with the feeders into New York, the factories around the Meadows, on the west side of the Meadows in Arlington, Kearny, and places like that. It may have been I just decided I didn't want to commute all my life—nothing any more substantial than that. Or maybe it was something I read. None of my family had ever before me been Navy, so I really don't know.

Paul Stillwell: Did you go to any sort of cram school before you took the entrance exam?[*]

Admiral Wylie: Yes. In January I went down to Bobby Werntz's in Annapolis.[†] I think my recollection is the exams were in February, and I was there for about six weeks. It was our congressman—whatever his name was, I haven't the faintest idea—had been the battalion deputy fire chief in Newark. He got elected to Congress. For reasons not known to me, he held a competitive exam, which was also the entrance exam. So that worked out very nicely. I was a youngster, I think, as a midshipman, when he came up again for election.[‡] He lost by one vote. This would have been November of whenever. They impounded the ballots, and there was a great argument. Father sent me the clippings out of the newspaper. They finally opened the vault in the county courthouse the following April, and all the ballots were gone, so he went back to being deputy battalion fire chief. This was a pretty sleazy political arena, as you probably know, then and now.

---

[*] "Cram school" was the term used for a preparatory school that covered the type of material that prospective cadets and midshipmen were likely to encounter on service academy entrance examinations.
[†] Robert Lincoln Werntz graduated from the Naval Academy in the class of 1884 and subsequently resigned his commission in June 1890. He then set up his preparatory school in Annapolis for prospective midshipmen and operated it for many years prior to his death in 1931.
[‡] A midshipman in his or her first year is called a plebe; second year, youngster or third classman; third year, second classman; fourth year, first classman. Actually, Wylie was probably in the early part of his second-class year during the congressional elections in November 1930.

Paul Stillwell: That's when Frank Hague was the boss.*

Admiral Wylie: He was over in Jersey City. Father, looking for an appointment for me, had gone over and called on somebody in that apparatus in Jersey City. The guy looked at him and said, "Mr. Wylie, you can't afford this appointment, not from this district." It was just as simple as that.

Paul Stillwell: Had you had a good foundation in school so that you were pretty well ready for the exams?

Admiral Wylie: Yes. The particular high school I went to, I had—my recollection is three years of Latin, three years of French, differential equations, certainly plane and, I think, solid geometry—the sort of things kids get in college these days. Of course, one result of that was that when I got to the Naval Academy I just coasted. I damn near bilged out the end of my youngster year when I finally got to something I hadn't had before. Then I had to go to work. But, yes, it was an education not now found in public schools.

Paul Stillwell: Was this in Newark itself?

Admiral Wylie: It was in Newark. The high school was Barringer, and I suspect it's all black now, but I don't know this. I haven't been back. Walked two miles. They had sidewalks, and it wasn't like this island, where there are no sidewalks.† That way you save the carfare; you got to keep it. A two-mile walk wasn't much.

Paul Stillwell: What are your recollections on arriving at the Naval Academy and starting plebe summer?

---

* Frank Hague (1876-1956) served as mayor of Jersey City, New Jersey, from 1917 to 1947. He was famous for saying, "I am the law in Jersey City." He had firm control of the Democratic Party politics in his local area, and he had clout on the national level as well. He was a member of the Democratic National Committee for more than 20 years.
† Newport, Middletown, and Portsmouth are all located on Rhode Island, a small island that is part of the state by the same name.

Admiral Wylie: Absolute bewilderment. Nothing notable. Nice kids. I was younger than most and was sort of tagging along for most of my four years. I had just turned 17, and a year or two years at that age is a gulf. Most of my class were 18 or 19, some 20, a few 23 or 24 illegally. But most of my time at the Naval Academy I watched those old guys. You know what I'm trying to tell you. I just had a lot of fun. I'd like to start over.

Paul Stillwell: Did the discipline require any adjustments?

Admiral Wylie: No, I don't think so. It was expected, where it might not be now. It was vastly more rigorous, I'm sure, than it is now, but nothing abnormal. I didn't even french out until my first class year.[*]

Paul Stillwell: What took you so long?

Admiral Wylie: I was a baby. I was a kid, you know, younger. There were half a dozen of them younger than I am, but not much more than that.

Paul Stillwell: What was the attraction for frenching out?

Admiral Wylie: Well, you have to remember this was Prohibition, and there was—I don't even remember his name, some Italian had a place where he sold dago red wine.[†] It was real hot stuff to go in there and sit around the table and drink that dumb stuff.

Paul Stillwell: What do you remember about Admiral Hart as superintendent?[‡]

---

[*] "French out" is midshipman slang for leaving the Naval Academy without authorization.
[†] The 18th Amendment to the Constitution was ratified in 1919 and went into effect in 1920, prohibiting the consumption of alcoholic beverages in the United States. The Volstead Act, enacted by Congress in 1919, spelled out the penalties for violations. In December 1933 the ratification of the 21st Amendment to the Constitution repealed the 18th Amendment and thus ended national prohibition.
[‡] Rear Admiral Thomas C. Hart, USN, was superintendent of the Naval Academy from May 1931 to June 1934. His oral history is in the Columbia University collection.

Admiral Wylie: Very rigorous, wore very high, stiff collars, and somehow or other, I had the wit to admire him. I wasn't real keen on the commandant, who was a Captain Snyder.* As midshipmen, we didn't think—well, I don't know how to say it. Never mind. But we all respected Admiral Hart. He was rigorous, but you didn't have to outguess what he'd do; you knew. This makes it very easy.

Paul Stillwell: Were there temptations to beat the system?

Admiral Wylie: For me not too many. Not too many. I'm probably one of the few people of my class that never had any time on the ship, the Reina Mercedes.†

Paul Stillwell: How did you avoid that?

Admiral Wylie: I guess I was too scared to be bold. I got little demerits. I never got big demerits. The little ones just piled up, but not the big ones.

Paul Stillwell: How much hazing or indoctrination and so forth was there from the upper classmen when you were there?

Admiral Wylie: Well, whatever there was, it was perfectly normal. I was never mistreated. I was never maltreated. I don't know any of my contemporaries who were. Whatever the system, we accepted it. Sure, we had to leap around every now and then, do some tricks every now and then. Did anybody ever tell you how you flush a toilet sitting at the dining room table?

Paul Stillwell: No, I haven't heard that one.

---

* Captain Charles Philip Snyder, USN, served as the Naval Academy's commandant of midshipmen from 1928 to 1931.
† USS Reina Mercedes (IX-25), captured during the Spanish-American War, served as a station ship at the Naval Academy from 1912 to 1957. Until 1940, midshipmen being punished for various disciplinary infractions slept and took meals on board the ship but continued to go to classes ashore.

Admiral Wylie: Well, you just go around and around and slide over the table. Visualize it. These things are not onerous.

Paul Stillwell: I've heard about sitting down when there's no chair.

Admiral Wylie. Sit on infinity. Of course. I think probably the most destructive thing occurred in the mess hall. At that time it was large, and tables were down each side. They had some pillars down the central aisle, I guess perhaps two feet in diameter. When the stewards brought out the meals on trays, they used to swing around these pillars, you know, when they had to make a turn. So they were bound in, I guess, about two feet of brass around the circumference. And the meanest of all tricks was to butter them.

Paul Stillwell: They'd go sliding and keep on sliding.

Admiral Wylie: Yes. But I never had to butter it. It was a very noisy tray load that hit the deck when that happened. That was a serious offense. I don't remember my table ever doing that. This is irrelevant.

Paul Stillwell: No, it depends on what somebody's interested in. It's hard to predict that. What do you remember about the academics?

Admiral Wylie: Well, once I almost bilged out in chemistry. I came to my senses and started to study, because from then on it was stuff that I hadn't had in high school. I don't know where I stood—about 100, I guess, from 450—respectable, certainly not noteworthy.[*]

Paul Stillwell: How intense was the competition among the members of the class?

Admiral Wylie: Everybody just about did his best. I have a notion that, say, up among the top 10 or 15, there was competition and rivalry, but the rest of us, we just chugged

---

[*] Of the 421 graduates in the Naval Academy class of 1932, Wylie was number 95 in the final standings.

along and did our homework and recited on schedule. I don't remember any intense competition other than the top 10 or 15 people in any class.

Paul Stillwell: Who are some of the members of the class you particularly remember?

Admiral Wylie: I've got a lot of friends in that class. It was probably the most undistinguished class that ever went to the Naval Academy, certainly in this century. No notable people, any of them. Lloyd Mustin has done very well.[*] Corky Ward did very well before he died.[†] Bryan did very well before he died, but he'd already had four years of college.[‡] God knows how old he was when he came in.[§] He was a very close friend, and I was very fond of him. But other than that, we just didn't have many notable people. Perfectly normal, perfectly nice.

Last class, I guess, before the Depression.[**] It was not fashionable to go to the Naval Academy or the Military Academy when I went. See, this was before the Depression, and all of the people with whom I grew up went off to college and sort of looked down their nose at anybody who wanted to be in the services. So we were the last class before the Depression. Maybe that's why there are no notable people in our class.

Paul Stillwell: I hadn't heard that theory before.

Admiral Wylie: It sort of makes sense, doesn't it?

Paul Stillwell: Well, sort of.

Admiral Wylie: Yes, but I just don't know.

---

[*] The oral history of Vice Admiral Lloyd M. Mustin, USN (Ret.), is in the Naval Institute collection.
[†] The oral history of Admiral Alfred G. Ward, USN (Ret.), is in the Naval Institute collection.
[‡] Rear Admiral Louis A. Bryan, USN, was on active duty at the time of his death in 1966.
[§] Bryan was born 17 October 1908.
[**] Following the crash of the New York Stock Exchange in late October 1929, the United States was plunged into the Great Depression, from which it did not recover until the nation geared up for World War II at the beginning of the 1940s. The Depression was marked by high unemployment and many business failures.

Paul Stillwell: Those people that started college in 1928 still had to have some means to finish the job after the Depression started.

Admiral Wylie: The Depression was the autumn of '28.

Paul Stillwell: Twenty-nine.

Admiral Wylie: Was it? Then we weren't the last class. We went in in the spring of '28 and graduated in 1932. So there was one more class after us, and that was the poor, benighted '33 class that all didn't get commissioned, and yet they had a lot more notable people—people notable in later life—than we did.* I don't know why. So there goes my theory.

Paul Stillwell: What extracurricular activities were you involved in?

Admiral Wylie: I tried crew, and I couldn't make it, so I became the manager so I could go to Poughkeepsie.

Paul Stillwell: What was the attraction in Poughkeepsie?

Admiral Wylie: That's before your time. You don't know. But they had the four-mile race every spring at Poughkeepsie. That was the intercollegiate crew event other than the Harvard-Yale race. They didn't go to Poughkeepsie, but everybody else did. I was too big for the lightweights and not good enough for the heavyweights, so I became the manager and got to go to Poughkeepsie. It's just that simple. Looking back, I haven't the faintest idea why, but I just wanted to.

Paul Stillwell: What were the duties of a manager?

---

* As an economy measure, in 1933 only the top half of that year's Naval Academy graduating class received Navy and Marine Corps commissions the year of graduation. Some members of the class were subsequently commissioned in 1934 and 1935. Still others joined the reserve and served on active duty in later years. And some were commissioned in other branches of the service.

Joseph C. Wylie, Interview #1 (5/21/85) – Page 9

Admiral Wylie: Lord, I don't even remember. You sort of bustled and made sure the towels were out or something, you know. It really wasn't much of a job.

Paul Stillwell: But it got you to go along.

Admiral Wylie: Yes, yes.

Paul Stillwell: Are there any of the instructors or the duty officers whom you particularly remember?

Admiral Wylie: Admiral Wright was a battalion commander then as a three-striper—Jerauld Wright, not that idiot of November of '42.* Beany Jarrett was a battalion commander; he was a little bit eccentric.†

Paul Stillwell: Tisdale was there also, wasn't he?

Admiral Wylie: He was the commandant, and I think Commander Thebaud was the executive officer.‡ No, that's when I came back as the duty officer, which I thoroughly enjoyed. I went kicking and screaming: "I don't want to go to the Naval Academy. The last thing I want to do is be in the executive department." I've seldom had as much pleasure. Skip now and go to that.

Well, for one year of my two, that is, '39 to '40, I was a company officer. From '40 to '41 I was assistant to the executive officer, who was Commander Thebaud, whom

---

* In 1934-35 Commander Jerauld Wright, USN, served in the executive department of the Naval Academy as battalion officer of the first battalion. As a four-star admiral he later served as Supreme Allied Commander Atlantic and Commander in Chief Atlantic Fleet from 1954 to 1960. Rear Admiral Carleton H. Wright, USN, was Commander Task Force 67 in the Battle of Tassafaronga, off Guadalcanal the night of 30 November-1 December 1942. In that battle the Japanese used torpedoes to sink the heavy cruiser Northampton (CA-26) and knock the bows off the cruiser New Orleans (CA-32) and Minneapolis (CA-36).
† Lieutenant Commander Harry Bean Jarrett, USN, was in the Naval Academy's executive department in the late 1930s. The frigate Jarrett (FFG-33) was named in his honor.
‡ Captain Mahlon S. Tisdale, USN, served as the Naval Academy's commandant of midshipmen in 1941-42. Commander Leo H. Thebaud, USN, was executive officer in the period shortly before the beginning of World War II.

I admired. Before I left in the summer of '41 we went to one of the spring parades. I recall walking back with him after the parade. I said, "They looked real good today, Commander."

He said, "Yes, take a good look at them, because 10% of them will be dead in five years." And that was the first realization I had that we were going to be in this war, etc. I was really quite naïve.

Paul Stillwell: I interviewed Commander Paul Backus, who was in '41, and he particularly remembered Thebaud as being a patient and understanding man, and he said the midshipmen had a lot of affection for Uncle Beany Jarrett.[*]

Admiral Wylie: Yes. Uncle Beany was a little eccentric. The then-Commander, later flag officer, Thebaud was pure 19th century, with a handkerchief either in his sleeve or his pocket. A gross sin was your hands in any pocket. He was just about 50 years too late for his disposition. I just loved him.

When I was commandant in Boston, one of his children or nephew, I don't know—children, I think—came and said that he and Mrs. Thebaud were having a 50th wedding anniversary very soon.[†] He had lived in that big house in Boston.[‡] I caught the drift of it and invited them to have the 50th wedding anniversary reception in the commandant's house in Boston. That gave a great deal of pleasure to be able to do that. He spent his summers somewhere up on the St. Lawrence, on the Canadian far side at one of those enormous hotel-type places, 19th century hotels that the CP or the CNR built, near Quebec.[§]

Paul Stillwell: He literally wrote the book on leadership.[**]

Admiral Wylie: I guess so. I enjoyed working for him. I admired him tremendously.

---

[*] See the Naval Institute oral history of Commander Paul H. Backus, USN (Ret.).
[†] As a rear admiral, Wylie served as Commandant First Naval District from December 1968 to November 1972.
[‡] Rear Admiral Thebaud served as Commandant First Naval District from July 1949 to February 1952.
[§] CP—Canadian Pacific; CNR—Canadian National Railroad.
[**] Leo H. Thebaud, Naval Leadership, With Some Hints to Junior Officers and Others; a Compilation by and for the Navy, First Edition (Annapolis: U.S. Naval Institute, 1924).

Joseph C. Wylie, Interview #1 (5/21/85) – Page 11

Paul Stillwell: Captain Vossler was the commandant, wasn't he?[*]

Admiral Wylie: I don't remember. I know Captain Vossler was there, but I can't even see him in my mind's eye. I just don't know.

Paul Stillwell: Are there any professors or instructors that you remember from the time you were a midshipman?

Admiral Wylie: Not really. I just can't. I can remember incidents. Here was some drunk in the ordnance department whose name—if I ever knew it, I've forgotten it—who surprised us one morning by being all bruised and battered. He looked up and said, "If you think I ran into a steamroller, I did." And he went back to his book, and we just sat there for an hour. We read it in the paper later. But nobody in particular. Just sort of dim, you know. It was all just admirable.

Paul Stillwell: Are there any other incidents that come to mind?

Admiral Wylie: I was with the first class, I think, that gave a football cheer for the Pope. Have you encountered this one before?

Paul Stillwell: Admiral Foley told me that Jack Lamade was the ringleader on that.[†]

Admiral Wylie: Yes. I'm not R.C. We went to Naples, and, of course, there were organized trips to Rome, and those of us who had the wit to go went. It was good for our little souls. But when we heard we were going to have an audience, we were a little bit afraid, because it had been organized, obviously, for the Catholics. So we stood in the back of the room. When the cheerleader jumped up, we were horrified. We didn't know

---

[*] Captain Francis Alfred L. Vossler, USN, served as the Naval Academy's commandant of midshipmen in 1940-1941.
[†] This incident is recounted in more detail in the Naval Institute oral history of Rear Admiral Francis D. Foley, USN (Ret.), a Naval Academy classmate of Admiral Wylie. Midshipman John D. Lamade, USN, was a Naval Academy cheerleader. The trip to the Vatican was in the summer of 1929.

what was going to happen, but we later figured out somebody had made these arrangements beforehand. That was for Pius XI, and it was a four-N Pius XI, just as simple as that.*

Paul Stillwell: What do you recall about the midshipman cruises you went on?

Admiral Wylie: Hammocks. I have one classmate, now dead. That morning we went to the Vatican, he got up—we had discovered Maca Machristi, which is a very heady wine, the night before. My God, we were 18 years old. Well, never mind.

Paul Stillwell: Go ahead.

Admiral Wylie: Well, he missed breakfast and tried to find some orange juice, and he finally did in a bar down the street. And what he didn't know was the guy thought if you have orange juice you put gin in it. So his head was spinning again.

One of the spaces in the Vatican through which we were led—it was not the Sistine Chapel, but it had urns around it, about four feet high. This fellow just went head first into an urn; he threw up.

But the more interesting part was after the audience with Pius XI, which was very impressive—this was a very impressive man—roughly in the center of St. Peter's there is a crypt, and there are stairs that go down from different directions. They had red ropes; you know, you're not supposed to go down. My classmate couldn't see very well, for one reason or another, and so he just stepped over the rope and went down to see what was down there. Pretty soon the attendants tried to get him out of there by shouting, and he got scared. They came down one way, and he went out another, you know, and started to run towards the west door.

The midshipmen then were not allowed to wear rubber heels, so you could hear these heels on the marble tile. Just as he got to the west end, the main door swung open, and I guess it was Captain Ellis—I don't remember the name of the admiral commanding

---

* The Pope at the time was Pius XI, head of the Roman Catholic Church from 1922 to 1939. The four-N cheer was as follows: "Na-vy! Na-vy! Na-vy! N-N-N-N. A-A-A-A. V-V-V-V. Y-Y-Y-Y. Na-vy! Fight, team, fight!"

the midshipmen's squadron.* It was the official party, and they came in. My classmate stood at attention, saluted, and slid right through them. They parted to let him through. Well, these are dumb things.

Paul Stillwell: What was the reason for the prohibition on rubber heels?

Admiral Wylie: I don't know. I don't know. It really doesn't make sense, in retrospect, but I'm quite sure we were not allowed rubber heels.

Paul Stillwell: What ships were you in during the midshipman cruises?

Admiral Wylie: Utah and Arkansas, two of them.† The second class summer—I think ours was the first or second of what were then called the aviation summers. The class work consisted of what was probably pretty primitive theory of aerodynamics. The practical work was going out—really, in retrospect, it's horrifying—in what was called an F-5L.‡ It was a seaplane biplane with piano wires strung between the wings. We must have gone up 200 or 300 feet on those flights, crowd four or five midshipmen in the back, and you couldn't see out very well. That was our indoctrination to aviation. F-5L, I'm sure they were.

Paul Stillwell: Did aviation have any appeal for you at that point?

Admiral Wylie: Not particularly, no. If they had had helicopters, where you could fly low and see, I think I probably would have been more enchanted, because the sightseeing is good from a helicopter. But other than that, I don't know.

Paul Stillwell: Is there any shipboard experience that you remember from those cruises?

---

* Captain Hayne Ellis, USN, commanded the battleship Arkansas (BB-33) in 1929-30.
† USS Utah (BB-31) was commissioned as a Florida-class battleship 31 August 1911. USS Arkansas (BB-33), lead battleship of her class, was commissioned 17 September 1912.
‡ The F-5L flying boat was an improved foreign version of an aircraft originally designed by Glenn Curtiss. He put the U.S. Navy-designed F-5L into production in 1918. It was 49 feet long, wingspan of 104 feet, gross weight of 13,600 pounds, a top speed of 90 miles per hour, and a range of 830 statute miles. It could be armed with six to eight .30-caliber machine guns and four 230-pound bombs.

Admiral Wylie: I think it was our first-class cruise a man named Wilkins had a submarine he was going to take to the North Pole.* There was a lot of flail in the newspaper about it. He left the United States before the midshipman cruise did, broke down in the mid-Atlantic. The Wyoming had to take him in tow and took him probably to Southampton. We felt very sorry for the people in the Wyoming, because they were several days late getting to wherever we went, Copenhagen. The cruises were much better then.

Paul Stillwell: You mean in terms of liberty ports?

Admiral Wylie: Sure. My two cruises—one to the Mediterranean and one to Northern Europe—kids don't get all that gentle cruising now.

Paul Stillwell: How was it as a learning experience for you?

Admiral Wylie: I'm sure it was good. Yes, I enjoyed it. I liked being a sailor. I started sailing when I was about eight, down off Barnegat Bay, and I enjoyed going to sea. Yes, I liked being on the water.

Paul Stillwell: Anything else from your Naval Academy years that particularly stands out for you?

Admiral Wylie: Not particularly, no. I enjoyed it.

Paul Stillwell: You got your education, if not your degree.

---

* Sir Hubert Wilkins was a noted British explorer. In 1931 he attempted operations in the Arctic in an ice-cutting submarine named Nautilus. As the USS O-12 (SS-73), she had been commissioned by the U.S. Navy in 1918. She was decommissioned in 1924 and struck from the Navy List in 1930. She foundered and in mid-June of 1931, had to be rescued by the USS Wyoming (BB-32), and was towed to Queenstown, Northern Ireland. After her ill-fated service as a civilian submarine, the Nautilus was returned to the Navy and sunk in a Norwegian fjord on 20 November 1931.

Admiral Wylie: Yes, yes. I have a notion in the late '30s, when the Congress authorized the Naval Academy to give degrees, bachelor of science, B.S., probably electrical, but I don't know this—that that may have been retroactive, you know. Those of us who got the commission, we came in for it. None of us ever thought about anything else. But I don't know anything more than that.

Paul Stillwell: It's interesting that you didn't have a really strong predisposition to the Navy. You just sort of went along with events.

Admiral Wylie: Yes. Well, I guess I didn't want to commute to New York, and I liked being on the water. As I say, I sailed a snake box from the time I was about eight to prove that I could swim all right, and it was safe. And all the summers I spent before the Naval Academy on Barnegat Bay, mostly sailing, some fishing. But I just enjoyed being on the water. Maybe that was the genesis.

Paul Stillwell: How, then, did your orders to the Augusta come about?*

Admiral Wylie: We put in for ships by type and perhaps by name, but, anyway, I put in for a cruiser and got Augusta. She was on the West Coast from the summer of 1932 until late spring of '33, when she went to China. We stayed aboard, six or seven of us out of my class. Because they didn't usually send junior ensigns to the Asiatic Fleet, but we went because we were already in the ship, and there was a fairly high turnover in the rest of the wardroom. Retrospectively, I guess a lot of the people didn't want to go to China, and so we had a lot of new people. We were the junior class on board Augusta for four years. We became jaygees, but we were still the junior class on board.†

---

* USS Augusta (CA-31), a Northampton-class heavy cruiser, was commissioned 30 January 1931. She had a standard displacement of 9,050 tons, was 600 feet long, 66 feet in the beam, and had a draft of 16 feet. Her top speed was 33 knots. She was armed with nine 8-inch guns and eight 5-inch guns. Because she was configured as a flagship, she frequently performed that function, both before and during World War II. She was eventually decommissioned on 16 July 1946.
† Jaygee—lieutenant (junior grade). In that era promotion to jaygee was customarily three years after being commissioned as an ensign.

Paul Stillwell: That's unfortunate, because there's no George to push things on to.[*]

Admiral Wylie: That's right, that's right. But that was fun, that cruise in the Asiatic Fleet.[†] I was out there three years. I can't really communicate with my own children on what it was like, because those were the last days of the Pukka Sahib.[‡] You're younger than my children. I can give you cues.

Whenever we went ashore, we normally carried a cane, a walking stick. The reason? If you carried it, the coolies would never jostle you, because you had the capacity to bang the cane down on a bare foot. Now, I never knew anybody who did it, but you had the stick, so you didn't get jostled by barefoot coolies.

In Shanghai, which, of course, was the largest of the ports, you didn't carry money ashore unless you were going to the dog races, the horse races, or the jai alai, where you need money to bet. Everything else, you'd just sign a chit for, unless they knew you, in which case you didn't have to sign a chit. The chits came out to the ship. We had Chinese stewards. The stewards paid them. Presumably, they took a cut. Then at payday, after you got your money, your steward would come up and say, "$40.00, Mr. Wylie." You never checked. And so you'd give him 40 bucks. That's the amount of chits he'd paid.

Four of us—Waters, Moncure, and one other ensign, classmates—two summers in Tsingtao, that would be the summer of '34 and the summer of '35, rented a cottage on the beach at Tsingtao.[§] On the beach—I mean, it was across the road by the beach, a perfectly normal, standard, probably German-built, four-bedroom house: living room, dining room, kitchen downstairs, four bedrooms upstairs. That was our house for the summer. It cost us a total of $28.00 U.S. That's $7.00 apiece a month, and that included the 11 servants that came with the house. My kids, they know I'm telling the truth, but they can't—you can't either.

---

[*] "George" is the traditional nickname for the junior ensign on board a given ship.
[†] The Augusta relieved her sister ship Houston (CA-30) as Asiatic Fleet flagship at Shanghai, China, on 9 November 1933.
[‡] "Sahib" means European spoken to or of by Indians; "pukka" means proper.
[§] Ensign Odale D. Waters, Jr., USN; Ensign Samuel P. Moncure, USN. The oral history of Waters, who retired as a rear admiral, is in the Naval Institute collection.

Paul Stillwell: I believe you.

Admiral Wylie: Yes, believe me, but this is a different world.

Paul Stillwell: Indeed it is, and so was your pay much lower too.

Admiral Wylie: One hundred five dollars a month. We were rich. We drank Peter Dawson Scotch, because that was less expensive than beer. Peter Dawson was 95 cents a quart, and the beer, even Japanese beer, cost more than that.

Paul Stillwell: Who was your first skipper on Augusta

Admiral Wylie: Oh, I was lucky. My first captain was Captain Joe Richardson, and he was relieved about May by Captain Royal Ingersoll, and he apparently didn't want to go to China, so Captain Nimitz joined the ship and took us to China.[*] He was aboard for three years, except for the last month before I was detached, there was a Captain Gygax.[†] He became a flag officer too. I came home, went to a destroyer under Commander Carney.[‡] So my first four captains were Richardson, Ingersoll, Nimitz, and Carney. You wonder I thought it was a good Navy?

Paul Stillwell: Four out of those five became four-star admirals.

Admiral Wylie: Oh!

Paul Stillwell: What are your individual remembrances of each of those? Richardson, for example, is always portrayed as a very avuncular man.

---

[*] Captain James O. Richardson, USN, commanded the heavy cruiser Augusta from the ship's commissioning on 30 January 1931 to 20 May 1933. Captain Royal E. Ingersoll, USN, commanded the Augusta from 20 May 1933 to 16 October 1933. Captain Chester W. Nimitz, USN, commanded the Augusta from 16 October 1933 to 12 April 1935. Richardson and Ingersoll became four-star admirals; Nimitz became a five-star admiral.
[†] Captain Felix X. Gygax, USN, who eventually became a rear admiral.
[‡] Commander Robert B. Carney, USN, commanded the new destroyer Reid (DD-369) in 1936-37. From 1953 to 1955, as a four-star admiral, he was Chief of Naval Operations.

Admiral Wylie: He was. He was very kind to his JOs.* For instance, at one stage, as a pink-cheeked little fresh-caught ensign, I was the assistant navigator. He came in and watched me watching the navigator, then told the navigator, "You're relieved for 48 hours. I want this young man to do it." This sort of thing. He took no nonsense. I was, in a very, very distant way, quite fond of him.

Captain Ingersoll, later CinCLantFlt—I never worked near him, because we rotated departments, and I must have been rotated out of the department that would have had me on the bridge except as a watch-stander.† But he was a good and kind man. Captain Nimitz I loved dearly. I would like to correct the misapprehension. He was a gentle, soft-spoken man, but he was every bit as tough-fibered as Admiral King.‡

Paul Stillwell: What manifestations did you see of that?

Admiral Wylie: The best manifestation of it is the parade of two-star people through the South Pacific in the autumn of '42; they got one strike and out.§ But the leadership was something else. When I took Ault out to the Pacific in early autumn of '44, there were three or four ships went out together. I had the squadron commander embarked, and when we got to Pearl Harbor, I just told the commodore, "Let's go up and call on the commander in chief."

He said, "Oh, no, he's got too much to do."

So I got the guy from the next ship, one of my colleague captains, and telephoned the flag lieutenant, got an appointment, 11:00 o'clock, went up, and called. People shouldn't have been afraid of that. When we got in the office there, he had the map on the wall, and he started talking about what we were going to do. This included finishing

---

* JOs—junior officers.
† Admiral Royal E. Ingersoll, USN, served as Commander in Chief Atlantic Fleet from 1 January 1942 to 15 November 1944. He was promoted to four-star rank in July 1942.
‡ Admiral Ernest J. King, USN, served as Chief of Naval Operations from 26 March 1942 to 15 December 1945 and as Commander in Chief U.S. Fleet from 20 December 1941 to 2 September 1945; he was promoted to the rank of fleet admiral in December 1944. He was a man with a demanding, difficult demeanor.
§ Nimitz served as Commander in Chief Pacific Fleet and Pacific Ocean Areas, 1941-45. He was promoted from four-star admiral to five-star fleet admiral in December 1945.

off the Philippines, Iwo Jima, Okinawa, and the assaults on Kyushu and Honshu. He didn't even tell us not to mention this. Of course, these were the deepest-held secrets of the Pacific War. He just <u>knew</u> we'd never tell anybody.

I remember going back to my ship for lunch, and my commodore said, "What did you learn up there?"

I said, "I learned what we're going to be doing for the next year and a half."

He said, "What?"

I said, "I can't tell you."

Paul Stillwell: He wished he'd gone then.

Admiral Wylie: I never did. He knew we wouldn't. What I'm describing to you is the subtlest form of real leadership, just superb. A gentle man.

I remember calling on him as an ensign, putting on our best bib and tucker in Long Beach, just before we went up for a month in Bremerton, before we went to China.[*] He lived in Long Beach then, had a house. Mrs. Nimitz came to the door and said, "He's around on the side porch." We could hear a man with a stringed instrument—ukulele, banjo, guitar, something—singing one of the bawdiest songs I've ever heard, to himself, just happy, had a drink out there. When we came out there, he put this whatever it was down, got us a drink—but never vulgar, never.

Paul Stillwell: He has a reputation as a storyteller. Did you see this when he was commanding officer of the <u>Augusta</u>?

Admiral Wylie: I didn't, but don't forget, we were the other end of the ladder.

I do have a nice little note in Bremerton, just before we sailed for China. One of my classmates, a man named Robards, was a small-arms nut, so he wanted to buy a pistol or a rifle.[†] The second or third street up from the waterfront in Seattle at that time—this is 50-odd years ago—was where the hockshops were. We put on our old clothes, and we

---

[*] Puget Sound Navy Yard, Bremerton, Washington.
[†] Ensign William C. F. Robards, USN, who was also in the crew of the <u>Augusta</u>.

took the ferry over, and he either bought or didn't buy what he was after. Still mid-afternoon, we were standing on the street corner. At that time the IWW were very prominent, and there was a copy of The Daily Worker in a rack, a newsstand, on the corner of whatever—this second or third avenue or street.[*] We were looking at it, and some guy sidled up to us, asked us who we were, and he said he was a fisherman. I said I was a dragger or something, different kinds of fishermen. So some other fellow turned up and took Robards off to his meeting place, and I was taken off to my meeting place. We went on separate ferries back to Bremerton.

At breakfast we were just overcome. We better report all this Communist stuff to the captain, and after breakfast we'd get an appointment. So we asked the exec if we could please have an appointment to call on the captain.[†] This was summer, so we put on our whites, 10:00 o'clock appointment up at Captain Nimitz's office.[‡] The Marine ushered us in, and Captain Nimitz said, "You young gentlemen were tinkering with things far beyond your knowledge yesterday, weren't you?"

He told me where I had been, and he told my colleague where he had been before we even got a word in edgewise. What had happened was, the intelligence apparatus had been functioning properly and had spotted us and had reported to Captain Nimitz before we could even open our mouths up in his cabin. I've had great respect for the naval intelligence service ever since. But Captain Nimitz thoroughly enjoyed dumbfounding us. He later let us tell what had happened. Of course, it was identical to what had been reported to him promptly. His final words were, "Young gentlemen, don't take in things that you can't manage," or something like that.

Paul Stillwell: I take it he didn't hold that against you subsequently.

Admiral Wylie: I was awfully glad we had requested that audience, though.

---

[*] IWW—Industrial Workers of the World.
[†] Exec—executive officer.
[‡] There is a possible glitch with this story in that in the summer of 1933 Captain Ingersoll was still commanding officer of the Augusta.

Paul Stillwell: Sure. What do you remember about your experiences in the separate departments as you made the rounds about the ship?

Admiral Wylie: I wish kids had the same opportunity today. There isn't time enough. Six months engineering, six months gunnery, six months communication, six months something else—maybe deck, I don't know. For two years we were very thoroughly grounded in our profession. I wish kids today had that kind of opportunity. It was good. We grumped at the time, I'm sure.

Paul Stillwell: How much chance did you get to handle the ship, if any?

Admiral Wylie: Some, not much. I guess most of that opportunity went to the lieutenants, who were very senior fellows then. You know, it's all relative.

Paul Stillwell: They probably had 15 years in by that time.

Admiral Wylie: Could have been, yes. Most of them very able men, a couple of drunks—you know, a good cross-section.

Paul Stillwell: Do you remember anything of the social life in the United States before you went over to the Asiatic Fleet?

Admiral Wylie: No, except we all had automobiles, the most expensive of which cost $25.00 in San Pedro. I was in the San Pedro earthquake, sixth of March, 1933, quarter of 6:00 in the evening.

I had an Ingersoll watch; that was the dollar watch. I wanted a nice chain to go with it, you know, because you wore watch chains then on the vest. I went into a hockshop in San Pedro, bickering for a chain, and finally I told him why I wanted it. The guy had a watch with a chain attached, and we were looking at that. I told him I didn't want the watch. I would give him $5.00 or $6.00 for the chain, or whatever. Then the earthquake struck, and everything came off the hooks on the walls, you know, and we stood out in the street for about 15 minutes. Finally, the owner of the hockshop rushed back in, came back out with the watch and chain, and I got it for six bucks. Well, as it turned out, the chain eventually turned green, but the watch was an absolutely superb Hamilton, which must have cost, even then, $100.00, and I've still got it. My wife, after I married, later bought a gold chain to go with it.

But that evening, all of us, of course, went back to our ships, and that was the first time I had ever seen an emergency apparatus get organized and function, and it was superb, because every ship was very quickly detailed: send people ashore, so on and so forth. All the doctors, for instance, were mustered in an open park, where presumably the Marines had set up tents.

One of the things that happen in an earthquake is that it brings on premature births, women who are within a month or so of term. The doctors had contest to see who could get the most babies named after their ship. Well, it's kind of hard to name a baby "West Virginia." Our doctor from Augusta won hands down. You know, August and Augusta—easy.

My job, with perhaps four or five men, was a street four or five streets back from the waterfront, and it was mostly small brick stores, and brick, of course, goes first into rubble. We were looking for people who had been caught in the rubble. We did not find any. At one stage we found a caved-in store just chock-a-block with broken glass and bottles. Finally, one of the men with me found a small case with very shallow drawers, filled with every kind of wine, beer, and whiskey labels you could think of. What we had stumbled into was a bottle shop whose business was supplying bootleggers with bottles and labels. He lost his stock. Enough said. These are not relevant.

Has anybody, including Admiral Burke, talked to you about the special defense section in CominCh at the closing two months of World War II?[*]

---

[*] Admiral Arleigh A. Burke, USN, served as Chief of Naval Operations from 17 August 1955 to 1 August 1961. His oral history is in the Naval Institute collection. CominCh was the abbreviation used for Commander in Chief U.S. Fleet when Admiral Ernest J. King, USN, held that title from 1941 to 1945. He was promoted to the five-star rank of fleet admiral in December 1944.

Paul Stillwell: He talked about that briefly, an attempt to set up a defense against kamikazes.[*]

Admiral Wylie: That's right. And Admiral Lee, whom you mentioned earlier, had the seagoing counterpart of that in Casco Bay that never really produced anything.[†] I think it was the first unearthing of what was then called MTI, or moving target indication. Admiral Burke had collected a very interesting group of officers. He got one from every type, is what it amounted to. He had a submarine officer; he had a destroyer officer. I was a destroyer officer. He had a cruiser, he had a battleship and amphibious, a patrol plane guy, a fighter type, and a night fighter type, who was Bill Martin.[‡] Night fighters were new then. One Marine—I guess 12 or 14 officers, but one from each apparatus. I don't think we did any good at all before the war ended, and that, of course, removed the reason for being, and it broke up.

Having just two months before that come ashore, I went over to the Bureau of Personnel. I feel strongly about the schism between line officers, aviators, and so on, and offered to go to sea again as a carrier exec, which, of course, the aviators raised their hands in horror. I then offered to take a destroyer if they'd give me as exec a carrier aviator who'd never had shipboard duties and who was going to stay in the Navy. Of course, he'd lose his bloody flight pay, but the answer was no. So I hung around and found a place to hide in the Office of Naval Research and stayed there until the demobilization was over.

Paul Stillwell: Admiral Mustin was the gunnery and radar officer on Lee's staff there, Task Force 69.[§]

---

[*] Kamikazes were Japanese suicide aircraft that began showing up in the Philippines campaign in the autumn of 1944. The pilots attempted to crash their bomb-armed aircraft directly into American warships. Hundreds of them successfully hit their targets and inflicted great damage.

[†] In the summer of 1945 Vice Admiral Willis A. Lee, Jr., USN, commanded Task Force 69, which conducted anti-kamikaze operational tests in Casco Bay, Maine. The force evolved into the Operational Development Force and was later renamed Operational Test and Evaluation Force (OpTEvFor).

[‡] Commander William I. Martin, USN. The oral history of Martin, who retired as a vice admiral, is in the Naval Institute collection.

[§] In the summer of 1945, when Task Force 69 was doing its anti-kamikaze tests, Lloyd M. Mustin was a commander. See his oral history for details.

Admiral Wylie: Yes.

Paul Stillwell: He has provided a quite detailed description of the research up there and the MTI.

Admiral Wylie: I don't think anything really came out of it. There were whiffs of what might be useful. MTI, I think, would have been at the head of the list, to catch planes coming down over the hills at Kyushu and Honshu. But I don't recall anything else that was potentially useful had been unearthed. It was a frantic effort. The best estimates, as I recall it, were 50% casualties—ships, ships' companies, embarked troops, and troops ashore—from kamikazes. It would have been absolutely ghastly.

Paul Stillwell: One thing he mentioned that was a counterpart to the idea that you had dye-loaded projectiles to identify which ship was shooting, was putting different colored flak bursts in the antiaircraft shells to see which ship was coming closest to the plane.

Admiral Wylie: I didn't know that. I don't recall that. If I ever knew it, I've long since forgotten it. I didn't contribute a damn thing in those two months, except to get to know Bill Martin and become very fond of him.

Paul Stillwell: Back in the Augusta period there was the term "Asiatic sailor" that described a breed that was somewhat apart from the sailor back on the West Coast.

Admiral Wylie: Yes, they'd get transferred away from a ship coming back to the United States. Some of them had been out there 10 or 12 years.

Paul Stillwell: Did you inherit some of those when you got over there in Augusta?

Admiral Wylie: A couple, yes. One incident, not this. The difference between the paternalistic Navy under the Articles for the Government of the Navy and the postwar Uniform Code of Military Justice—at that time, it may still be so now—but if a man was over leave for 30 days, he would be declared a deserter, and his things were sent home.* We had a couple. I know one day I was a JO of the deck, moored in Shanghai, and a man who had been gone for—pick a number, 40, 45 days—came up the accommodation ladder. And the boatswain's mate said, "Oh, God, here comes Chiselinski back."

I started out, and the officer of the deck, a lieutenant, pushed me back, went over, looked this man up and down, and said, "I've never seen him before in my life. That's not Chiselinski. Take him back ashore." That solved it. There was a guy without a passport, without a national identity. He paid. We will never know what happened to him, whatever his name was.

Paul Stillwell: And probably no money to get anywhere either.

Admiral Wylie: That's right. But we finished the paperwork. We weren't going to horse around with him.

At that time chief petty officers brought up junior officers, and my mentor was a chief signalman named Struckus. This is flavor.

Paul Stillwell: Flavor is useful.

Admiral Wylie: Struckus was a fine chief petty officer, and in Shanghai once he was half a day late, and I didn't do anything. Then the next week he was, say, a day late coming back. I said, "Chief Struckus, we can't do this anymore."

He said, "No, sir."

Then a week after that, he was three days late. And when he came back, I said, "Chief Struckus, I've got to put you on report this time."

He said, "Oh, no, sir, you don't want to do that." He said, "If you put me on report, I'll have to go to mast, and if I go to mast, Captain Nimitz will have to disrate me. And he don't want to disrate me, because I'm a good chief signalman."

"What the hell do you want me to do?"

---

* Following the unification of the U.S. armed forces in 1947, a new Uniform Code of Military Justice (UCMJ) was enacted for all the services and put into effect on 31 May 1951.

He said, "Sir, you restrict me for three months." So I restricted him for three months. There's a relationship here and a state of mind that I don't know whether exists today. I doubt it.

Paul Stillwell: Well, it has its civilian counterpart in what's called plea bargaining.

Admiral Wylie: Yes, but there's more to it than that. It's a very real and very effective paternalism that the UCMJ has certainly inhibited a great deal, because we had enormous latitude.

Paul Stillwell: And the chiefs had a great deal of latitude in their discipline.

Admiral Wylie: Sure, sure. It was in this flavor and this aura that I was brought up, and my contemporaries, of course, and it was different after the Doolittle bit. Zumwalt could never have been CNO, and he could never have issued those bloody Z-grams under the paternalistic world of pre-World War II.* It would have been impossible. It wouldn't have worked.

Paul Stillwell: That was a time, also, when not very many Navy men had families.

Admiral Wylie: That's right. There were very few married bluejackets. They were magnificent. Most of them were high school graduates. Lots of them had dropped out of college. This was Depression. I suspect most of them became officers in World War II, but, goodness, we had a lot of talent in the general mess.† The Navy was very selective then, and we got awfully good men. They're the ones that won World War II.

Paul Stillwell: The Navy was also very small then.

---

* Admiral Elmo R. Zumwalt, Jr., USN, served as Chief of Naval Operations from 1 July 1970 to 29 June 1974. Z-grams were consecutively numbered policy directives from Zumwalt and his staff that attempted to deal with such issues as enlisted rights and privileges, equal opportunity, and Navy families. Junior personnel viewed them much more favorably than did their seniors. See U.S. Naval Institute Proceedings, May 1971, pages 291-298. Admiral Wylie was close to retirement when Zumwalt became CNO.
† In this context, the term "general mess" is not a derogatory term. It refers to the shipboard dining compartment for enlisted men below the level of chief petty officer.

Admiral Wylie: Yes.

Paul Stillwell: People saw each other time after time.

Admiral Wylie: Yes, as an ensign I knew every captain on the West Coast, four-striper, by name, not by sight. It was a tight little club.

Paul Stillwell: What do you remember about the Marines on board ship?

Admiral Wylie: I remember Lewis Puller, whom I loved dearly.* He was a junior Marine. At one time, we played poker at night in the wardroom with kids, and Lewis would sit in occasionally. It took him about three days to earn his mess bill. Then he stayed level the rest of the month. He kept books. He stayed level. He never won more than his mess bill, a dollar or two more. He was gone for about six weeks, and when he came back he was a taciturn man, and he also enjoyed being taciturn. He knew what he was doing.

"Where you been, Lewis?"

"I've been down in Nicaragua."

"What did you go down there for?"

"We had to find a guy."

"Did you find him?"

"Yeah."

I'm compressing this, you see. He made us drag it out of him: "How did you find a fellow like that, Lewis?"

"Oh, you ask his friends."

We all expressed disbelief at that. He said, "Oh, yeah, they'll tell you anything."

"How do you do that, Lewis?"

---

* First Lieutenant Lewis B. "Chesty" Puller, USMC, was commanding officer of the Augusta's Marine detachment from 1934 to 1936. He was a highly decorated officer who later served in World War II and the Korean War. He eventually retired as a lieutenant general. The frigate USS Lewis B. Puller (FFG-23) was named in his honor.

He said, "Well, you know these little magneto-driven telephones?"

We said, "Yeah."

He held up his two fingers and said, "Every one of those guys has got cavities. They'll tell you anything."

Paul Stillwell: Was that when they went after Sandino?*

Admiral Wylie: I suspect so. I didn't know it at the time, but in retrospect it could well have been. You know about him. He had been in Haiti, in La Guardia-Seville, when he was a sergeant in the U.S. Marines. He was the commandant of La Guardia-Seville in Haiti.

In Manila one winter—one January, I guess, when we did all our gunnery practice in six weeks, so that we'd be free to act as the commander in chief's flagship the rest of the year—well, the first thing I must do is identify a wardroom conversation, which is a positive statement, a flat denial, and a bet. I walked into the wardroom after the movies one night, and Lewis Puller and Lloyd Mustin were just having a fist-banging argument. Lloyd Mustin's position was that you had to be born with a gift of some kind to shoot a rifle or pistol. Lewis Puller's position was, "I can take any dumb son of a bitch and teach him to shoot. I can even teach him," which was me, walking in the door. Well, there was $10.00 on it. So a couple of weeks later, when Lewis took his Marine detachment out to Fort McKinley to do their annual bit over the rifle range, I went. And, of course, I came back with a Marine expert rifle medal, and Lewis won his $10.00. That's my Lewis Puller ribbon.

Paul Stillwell: Do you know whether you really hit the target?

Admiral Wylie: You bet I did. You bet I did. Starting at 1,000 yards, thank you, and ending up offhand at 100. But we worked from morning light till dusk. Every one of his Marines was an expert; make no mistake about it.

---

* U.S. Marines were in Nicaragua almost continuously from 1912 to 1933. They were subject to raids by a rebel leader, General Augusto César Sandino, from whom the Sandinistas took their name. In 1934, after the U.S. Marines left, Sandino was murdered by national guardsmen while under a flag of truce.

I have another Puller story for you. I had Trever, which was a World War II DMS, converted four-piper, off Guadalcanal, I would guess January of '43.[*] I was summoned over to Camp Alligator, which was amphibious headquarters on Guadalcanal. I was told to please take some supplies and ammunition up around the northwest point of the island, because there was a Marine scouting detachment, which was going around the Japanese, and come out there. The substance of the conversation at Camp Alligator was, "He said he'd be there at midnight Tuesday, so maybe you better go up on Monday and check in, and again on Wednesday if he doesn't turn up. He said midnight, so you'd better go in about 10:30 and wait till 2:00 or something.

I "Yes, sirred" to all this. Finally I asked the name of the Marine, and it was Major Puller. I said, "Oh, Captain Doyle, I know him. He'll be on time. I'll go up Tuesday, midnight." Then I turned and left. Well, I was being cocky, of course. Well, I did. As a matter of fact, I took a couple of bottles of whiskey in. Lewis and I sat there, and we had a couple of drinks while the supplies came in. He was right on time. We had a flashlight rendezvous, you know, the boat and the thing. When they got all the supplies ashore, he took the two bottles of whiskey, gave them to his first sergeant, told him to take care of them till the next night, and move out. They just moved out.

Paul Stillwell: Captain Doyle was on Turner's staff, wasn't he?[†]

Admiral Wylie: Yes, he was the chief of staff. I've got another one on him in there. He was a very nice man and a very smart man. I thought he was older than God at the time, but obviously he wasn't. But he saved me a lot of trouble on another occasion, which is in one of the letters to my grandchildren. I won't bore you with it.

Paul Stillwell: What do you remember about the fleet commanders in chief out there on the China Station?

---

[*] On 7 August 1942, U.S. Marines invaded the islands of Guadalcanal and Tulagi in the Solomons chain as part of the first U.S. counteroffensive in the Pacific War. The primary purpose was to gain control of an airstrip on Guadalcanal and thus to prevent the Japanese from achieving control of the surrounding air and sea regions. The campaign was long and difficult before organized Japanese resistance finally ended on 9 February 1943.

[†] Captain James H. Doyle, USN, was on the staff of Rear Admiral Richmond Kelly Turner, USN, who was in command of the amphibious task force for the Guadalcanal operation.

Admiral Wylie: One of them was Murfin.* The one who was out there most of the time was Upham.† For instance, in autumn of 1934, he, as the U.S. representative to the centennial celebration of Melbourne, went down to Australia in Augusta; we went.‡ I was in communications then, which is why I saw the traffic.§

When we got somewhere, let us say, south of Guam, headed for Australia down through the Bougainville Straits area, the admiral sent a very nice, perfectly proper message to the Duke of Gloucester, who was in Suffolk or Sussex, one of the British County-class cruisers, then in the Indian Ocean.** He got back a very snotty reply, "I will inform His Royal Highness of the substance of your message. Signed Smith-Jones, equerry." Well, that first message from Admiral Upham was very nice. From that point on, he didn't ask the British anything. He told them forthright, flat out—no courtesy. He just matched snottiness with snottiness, because that was a very rude message, and he took no guff whatever. That impressed me. Admiral Upham was not a very prepossessing man—medium height, a little chubby, but he certainly rose in our estimation when he put the Duke of Gloucester and his equerry back down where they belonged.

We were both in Melbourne together three weeks, give or take, across the pier from each other. This was the biggest celebration that Melbourne had ever had. The Duke of Gloucester, by the way, was down there on approval to see if they'd take him as Governor-General, and they wouldn't. He was rejected. He finally got down there during World War II, but he was turned down on that occasion, we later heard from some of our friends.

---

* Admiral Orin G. Murfin, USN, served as Commander in Chief U.S. Asiatic Fleet from 4 October 1935 to 30 October 1936.
† Admiral Frank B. Upham, USN, served as Commander in Chief U.S. Asiatic Fleet from 18 August 1933 to 4 October 1935.
‡ The Augusta visited Melbourne from 29 October to 13 November 1934.
§ "Traffic" refers to the radio messages to and from the ship.
** Prince Henry, Duke of Gloucester (1900-1974) was the son of King George V, then Britain's reigning monarch. Two of the duke's older brothers later succeeded to the throne, King Edward VIII and King George VI. The Duke of Gloucester served as Governor-General of Australia from 1945 to 1947.

Anyway, Suffolk, Sussex—whichever it was, call it Suffolk—obviously had a wine mess. We did not. We were dry.* We didn't go anywhere on our own. We were assigned to two or three parties: afternoon, dinner, and post-dinner. The wardroom—white tie every night for dinner. Finally, Commander Whiting, later Admiral Whiting, who was the exec, put out a notice that no officer was to be called in the morning unless he had the watch.† All guests were to be off the ship by 5:00 A.M. If the second dog watch wanted to eat in the wardroom, he'd have to get into white tie; otherwise, he'd have dinner in his room.‡ We drew the crowds because—you'd never believe it—we had Brazilian coffee. All these people had ever had was that heavy Indonesian coffee, and we had light Brazilian coffee. Starting about 1:00 o'clock, our wardroom was full until it was cleared out at 5:00 in the morning.

The second day there—and I've got another Lewie Puller story in a minute, I'll give it to you—the second day or the first day, the Lord Mayor of Melbourne came down to call, and he must have found out we were dry. This was a novelty then. The next morning, there was a little shed at the head of the dock. That was the sly grog for the wardroom, a speakeasy.

One afternoon we had a reception on board. Lewis Puller was late. He had taken his rifle team off somewhere. A couple of us saw him go over the after brow down below and then come up on the forecastle, where the reception was. Commander Whiting saw him and ate him up right there at the hatch: "Late again, Puller," and so forth.

Then the next morning the Lord Mayor came down again. What had happened was that a ferry coming into mooring at Melbourne—in the ferry slip there had been a car waiting on the ramp, and it was fairly steep. The car's brakes had let go, and the car had gone into the water just as the ferry was entering the slip. Of course, the ferry backed down full. Somebody went in the water and got the three girls out of the car and got them up. Lewis had sworn his Marines to silence. He had done it.

---

* On 1 July 1914 a general order from Secretary of the Navy Josephus Daniels went into effect. It abolished the traditional wine messes on board U.S. Navy ships, resulting in a prohibition against drinking alcoholic beverages on board. The ban was relaxed in the 1980s to permit the serving of beer and wine--but not hard liquor—at official receptions on board.
† Commander Francis E. M. Whiting, USN.
‡ Dogging a watch means splitting it in half. Instead of a watch lasting from 4:00 P.M. to 8:00 P.M., there were two watches, 4:00 to 6:00 and 6:00 to 8:00, so watch standers would have an opportunity to get an evening meal.

The Lord Mayor came down, called on the admiral. The admiral sent for the chief of staff; the chief of staff sent for Captain Nimitz; Captain Nimitz sent for the exec; the exec sent for the fleet Marine officer; he sent for the ship's Marine, the major, and he sent for the sergeant. The sergeant wouldn't tell them anything. He had been told by Lewis to keep quiet. So finally they sent for Lewis, and he finally admitted he'd been the guy who had gone in front of the ferry, got the girls out of the car safely.

Paul Stillwell: Why didn't he want it known?

Admiral Wylie: He didn't like things known. He just didn't want all the fuss.

Paul Stillwell: Was this Red Whiting?

Admiral Wylie: Yes. He bawled me out once. He was standing on the forecastle. The ship was in that floating dry dock in Olongapo.[*] He was on the forecastle, and I was under one of the propellers in the base of the dry dock, and neither I nor anybody else missed a word. Oh!

Paul Stillwell: That was a generation of naval officers who didn't need a 1MC to be heard.[†]

Admiral Wylie: That's for sure. That's for sure. He was a good officer, though, but, boy, he was tough on his junior officers.

Paul Stillwell: He was skipper of the Massachusetts when she fired those projectiles that didn't explode over in North Africa.[‡]

---

[*] Olongapo is the town right outside the U.S. naval base at Subic Bay in the Philippines.
[†] 1MC—a ship's general announcing system.
[‡] Allied forces invaded Casablanca in French Morocco in November 1942. The French forces in the port resisted, so American ships, including the battleship Massachusetts (BB-59), bombarded the port.

Admiral Wylie: Yes. Well, I imagine that was duly reported. I don't think that special defense section that Commodore Burke ran really did anything useful. But you have Mustin on that, because he was in Admiral Lee's half of it, and he would have known much more than I. I'm not technical, by the way.

This is just an odd notice. I spent three and a half years as commandant in Boston. Why did I stay so long? I wouldn't give Zumwalt my vacancy.* About every six months he'd get somebody to call and ask when I was going to retire. Remember, he fired all those good three-star guys.

Paul Stillwell: Fired some four-stars too.

Admiral Wylie: Yes. But he took out a decade's worth of talent, that son of a bitch.

This won't help anybody, but somebody might find it useful. It took me about two months to figure out that the two most useful people on my staff in Boston were the lawyer and the public relations man. Nobody else really mattered. The result was, without going into details, we were never bested, either in the newspapers or in court by the ACLU, the Dr. Spock crew, that cabal of lawyers up there.† We won every bout, either in the newspapers or in the court. It was the PR man. And I'm not talking about a public relations man or an advertising man who's looking for ink. What I'm talking about—and I had to get rid of two before I got one to do this—who can see trouble down the road, figure out how to either avoid it or turn it to advantage or, at the least, minimize it. Enough said.

Paul Stillwell: I just wonder if there are any examples of cases you could give to illustrate that point?

---

* Rear Admiral Francis D. Foley, USN, whose oral history is in the Naval Institute collection, was a Naval Academy classmate of Wylie. Foley was commandant of the Third Naval District in New York when Wylie was in Boston. Foley also received letters asking him to retire, which he did not follow. According to Foley's aide, Jed Levine, Foley and Wylie made a game of calling each other on the telephone when the retirement requests came and making sounds to pretend they were tearing up the letters.
† ACLU—American Civil Liberties Union. Dr. Benjamin J. Spock, who had been a Naval Reserve medical officer in World War II, was a prominent pediatrician and author of the best-selling book Common Sense Book of Baby and Child Care. He was prominent in the anti-Vietnam War movement. In 1968 he was convicted on conspiring to counsel young men on how to avoid the military draft.

Admiral Wylie: Yes. The newspapers, except for The Globe and station WEEI, were very good to us, because they had a lot of World War II veterans on the staff. For instance, we received information one day that there was a gang of kids from one of the colleges—I forget, probably Harvard—coming down. They chained themselves to the mast on Constitution, and, of course, there was no sense in doing this unless you tell the news media, which they did.[*] So we figured how to handle that one, thanks to—we had a couple of Marines on board with those enormous cutters, you know, to cut the chain with. As soon as they'd lashed themselves up good, we'd cut them off, take them down to the other end of the yard. The newspapers asked if we were putting them in jail. We said, "Of course not. We're just detaining them. We've sent for their parents." That turned the whole thing around. One parent had to come all the way from Ohio to get his kid out of our detention cell. Do I communicate how to turn something to advantage?

Another time—of course, that was 1970, late '60s, early '70s—we had half a dozen Marines, for instance, up in the jug at Portsmouth, which was run by a very good Marine.[†] These were drug dealers out of Korea or someplace. Their cause had been taken up by the ACLU or somebody. They were going to march up there and demand to see them. So we figured out, thanks to the good PR man and the good lawyer—the lawyer found a new interpretation of the UCMJ. We could send them on their own down to Quantico.[‡] So we bought them all airplane tickets. And, of course, I telephoned the Marine general at the other end, and he almost had conniption fits. I had to go through it by the numbers to explain to him, "Look, if these guys get there, we're way ahead, because they're salvageable. If they don't get there, you're well rid of them, and you don't have to hold another court-martial." So he finally agreed, and we gave all those guys airplane tickets, rode them to Boston, and put them on a plane. Well, all but one did arrive. But the point is, Dr. Spock and all his people marched on Portsmouth and demanded to see these prisoners.

"Sorry, you can't see them."

---

[*] USS Constitution, a wood-hull frigate launched in 1797, gained fame in the War of 1812 as "Old Ironsides." To this day she is maintained at Boston as a commissioned ship of the U.S. Navy.
[†] At the time the Navy's main prison was at Portsmouth, New Hampshire. It has since closed.
[‡] Quantico, Virginia, is the site of a Marine Corps base.

And finally they had the wit to ask, "Why can't we see them?"

And we said, "They left Logan this morning, going down to Quantico."[*] And, of course, what that does is turn the whole newspaper account upside down. Do I communicate?

Paul Stillwell: You defanged them.

Admiral Wylie: Yes. What it really is is a poverty-stricken vocabulary that can't distinguish between selling soap and influencing the turn of events. They're quite different, and you need quite different talents. But, yes, that sort of thing. And we never lost a case, either in the newspapers or in the courts.

Paul Stillwell: How was it that Admiral Zumwalt had to ask you to retire, rather than just being able to tell you?

Admiral Wylie: He could tell a three-star guy to retire. The language is that three-stars are temporary. Unless there's a recommendation from the Navy to Congress, you revert back and retire at two-star. Two-stars are permanent once you get past the plucking board.[†] I don't even know whether that exists now. Maybe it's been legalized and called something else since they've got commodores. I guess it's promotion or continuation.

But it used to be in camera, a board. You never knew who got plucked. You just had to wait till you retired the next year. It was all very nicely handled. But, anyway, I don't know what the law is now, but at that time I could serve until my 62nd birthday. I didn't. I got out of my own volition six months, 12 months before that.[‡] But there was one way he could have done it. He could have sent me home awaiting orders, and I would at once have gone on half pay. But that's the only lever he's got, other than a court-martial for some offense. For permanent commission, two stars, I just wouldn't

---

[*] Logan is the name of the Boston airport.
[†] "Plucking board" is a nickname for the continuation board. After a group of flag officers has held flag rank a few years, the continuation board chooses which have to retire at that point and which can continue on active duty.
[‡] Admiral Wylie retired from active duty 1 July 1972. His 62nd birthday was 20 March 1973.

give him my vacancy. I guess petty, spiteful, stubborn, but too many good three-star guys had been clubbed, the ones I knew.

Paul Stillwell: I interviewed Admiral Hyland, who was CinCPacFlt, and he said he got a letter dated 1 July 1970, which was Zumwalt's first day in office, asking him to retire.*

Admiral Wylie: Oh, no. I didn't know that. Well, B. J. Semmes got the back of his corporate hand by way of that despicable Stansfield Turner, but that's neither here or there at the moment.†

Paul Stillwell: What else do you have in your notes?

Admiral Wylie: Boston, China. We've talked about the last days of the Pukka Sahib.

Two things. I mentioned that I went to work for—went up, and Admiral Tisdale sent me home.‡ In either late December of '42, January of '43 I got my first command, which was Trever, a converted four-piper, dirty old ship.§

In June one of the DesPac staff came down and started talking about how I was going up to the staff in Pearl Harbor for CIC.** I said I didn't know a goddamn thing about labor unions and wouldn't fool with them. And he explained to me that there had to be some kind of a combat operation aboard ship. Well, the background is that on the

---

* Admiral John J. Hyland, USN, who was serving as Commander in Chief Pacific Fleet, left that billet on 5 December 1970 and retired 1 January 1971. See Hyland's Naval Institute oral history.
† Vice Admiral Stansfield Turner, USN, a Zumwalt protégé, relieved Vice Admiral Benedict J. Semmes, Jr., USN, as president of the Naval War College on 30 June 1972. Semmes, who was a 1934 Naval Academy classmate of Admiral Hyland, retired 1 July 1972; his oral history is in the Naval Institute collection.
‡ Rear Admiral Mahlon S. Tisdale, USN, served as Commander Destroyers Pacific Fleet from 8 January 1943 to 2 January 1944 and as Commander Cruisers Pacific Fleet from 1 April 1943 to 2 January 1944.
§ USS Trever (DD-339), a Clemson-class destroyer, was commissioned 3 August 1922. Displacement was 1,308 tons, length 314 feet, and beam of 31 feet. Top speed was 35 knots. She was armed with four 4-inch guns, one 3-inch gun, and 12 21-inch torpedo tubes. She was reclassified as a high-speed minesweeper (DMS-16) on 19 November 1940. In the spring of 1942 she received an extensive overhaul that included removal of her 4-inch gun mounts and installation of light antiaircraft guns.
** CIC—combat information center.

13th of November, the action off Guadalcanal, I was in the charthouse.* I made a series of sketches of the radarscope, for what reason I can't to this day remember. I just had good sense, without realizing it, and made these sketches. They eventually got up to Pearl Harbor, and by that time, unbeknownst to me, people had begun to realize there was a vast amount of information that was not being properly correlated. So, to cut the long story short, I was detached from Trever and sent to Pearl Harbor. It's sort of lovely. I went in, paid my call on Admiral Tisdale, whom I had served at the Naval Academy. He gave me the old ho-ho-ho and said, "Wylie, glad to see you."

I said, "Goddamn it, Admiral, I'm not glad to be here. You took me away from my first ship."

He tried to calm me down and said, "I'll tell you what. I'll let you go in six months or when I'm detached, whichever is sooner."

And, being absolutely exhausted and tired, I said, "Admiral, will you put that in writing?" He sort of stared at me and sent for his chief yeoman, and he dictated it. Of course, when I went out of the office, all the other guys on the staff wanted the same thing. He said, "No, you didn't think of it. He did, and that's the only one I'm giving out."

Well, as it turned out, at Christmas I was down in Espiritu Santo. I had been sent out there to run a destroyer school, which was an odd school. I'll come back to the CIC later.

I was living in Dixie with Bill Cole, my former skipper in Fletcher, who was then Commander Destroyers SoPac.† The school was over in Aori Island and very interesting, no curriculum. The instructors—we had a gunnery, a communicator, an engineer, one of everything that a destroyer wardroom has—and they were all fresh out of ships that had just been in combat. What it was was a place for newly arriving ships to come over and talk and ask questions and get the feel of the business, no curriculum. It was probably

---

* On the night of 12-13 November 1943, off the island of Guadalcanal, a U.S. surface force comprised of five cruisers and eight destroyers was badly mauled by Japanese gunfire. For details see James W. Grace, The Naval Battle of Guadalcanal: Night Action, 13 November 1942 (Annapolis: Naval Institute Press, 1999). During the battle Wylie was executive officer of the destroyer Fletcher (DD-445), which was the last ship in the U.S. formation.
† Commander William M. Cole, USN, was the first commanding officer when the Fletcher was commissioned 30 June 1942. USS Dixie (AD-14) was a destroyer tender. SoPac—South Pacific.

useful for a very short period of time, and it probably was continued long after its usefulness had disappeared, but it was a school without a curriculum.

But, anyway, my job in Pearl Harbor was to write what later turned out to be a handbook for CIC. There was sonar information that was getting better with new machinery; there was radar information that was getting better and all that. So our job was to—what should a combat information center have in it, how should it be arranged, and how should it be managed? Well, the result was about a 25- or 30-page pamphlet, Destroyer CIC Handbook, or CIC Handbook for Destroyers. That was ready, I would guess, a month after I got up there, maybe six weeks. So we counted up the number of destroyers and the number of destroyers coming, and we figured two per ship and then copies for every division and squadron commander. Anyway, we printed 500 copies in the tender. Within six weeks, we had printed 15,000 copies for the USN and the RN.[*] That was my first bestseller.

Paul Stillwell: Pretty good numbers.

Admiral Wylie: When I finished that, Admiral Tisdale said, "Well, I told you when I'm detached or six months, and neither has come yet. I want you to go down and start a school in Espiritu Santo." And I was down there for a couple of months. Between Christmas and New Year's—I think this would have been 1943—it came over the schedules that Admiral Kauffman had relieved Admiral Tisdale.[†] Well, the next day, there came in a message addressed to Commander Wylie, the dean of the Coconut College. It wasn't "White Poppy" but whatever our code name was for Espiritu Santo. "Nominate relief. Detached immediately. Report to Admiral Tisdale in Fairmont Hotel, San Francisco."

Well, that baffled me. Two things. One is, by the time I got that, there was a destroyer standing in the channel, and I got the yeoman to get the name of the commanding officer, and I submitted that as the name of my relief. Whoever he was, he will never have forgiven me. Second, I finally figured out what Admiral Tisdale had

---

[*] RN—Royal Navy.
[†] Rear Admiral James L. Kauffman, USN, served as Commander Destroyers Pacific Fleet and Commander Cruisers Pacific Fleet from 2 January 1944 to 31 October 1944.

done. He'd given me a chance to get through Pearl Harbor without anybody knowing it, because they'd have snaffled me. I reported to him at the Fairmont, and he had a ship for me.

Paul Stillwell: So he was as good as his word.

Admiral Wylie: He kept his word. I loved him dearly. It took me a while to figure this. This is a funny. I later learned that the people in DesPac were looking for me. I had the wit to go up on an ATC, Air Transport Command, Air Force plane, and so I didn't get into the Navy system at Pearl Harbor. I finally got to San Francisco that way, and they never knew I went through. But that dear old man had certainly taken care of me.

The basic concept of CIC—we drew a square, and the horizontal line, that is, the front ship's line, we decided everything forward was current information, and everything back, that is, on the after bulkhead, for practical purposes was history. Now, what we're talking about here is the DRT, the dead-reckoning tracer, the polar plot of the air plot, the plot of the submarine thing. And up forward were the radarscopes and the sonar. We divided it fore and aft into air and surface. I forget which was which. So here would be the surface-search radar, that is, the Sugar George, and here would be the surface plot.* There would be the air-search radar, there would be the air plot, and in between them, back there would be the sonar information. It worked.

Paul Stillwell: How did you find a space in the ship to set this up, since they hadn't necessarily been designed that way?

Admiral Wylie: Screw the division commander out of his cabin. He got the captain's cabin. There was no other way to do it for ships already laid down. Later, by the time <u>Ault</u> came along, which was spring of '44, the CIC had been planned into the ship.

---

* Sugar and George were words used in the phonetic alphabet of the time. SG was the designation of one of the early surface-search radars.

Paul Stillwell: Of course, in these ships you're not going to have a division commander anyway, so it's no problem.

Admiral Wylie: Yes, but that worked. It worked pretty good. In retrospect, it's quite astonishing that nobody had ever done anything, either in the RN or USN, to collect all information in one place, except in the captain's noggin.

Paul Stillwell: Somebody had to think of it the first time.

Admiral Wylie: Well, that was what I was summoned to do, and it worked. Then I got another trip back to the United States to sell it to DesLant. I forget who DesLant was, but he was running the submarine war, and the most urgent thing on his agenda was a Pullman roomette equipment for the emergency cabin on the bridge, you know, with a bunk that would become a couch, and a washbasin, and a head that would come out of the wall. So our agreement was, he would support our CIC in Washington, and we would support his Pullman roomette, which was a vast improvement over the pipe bunk or something which we'd had in the sea cabin. So both destroyer forces were united, and the Bureau of Ships and the kibitzers in Washington really couldn't fight that when you have both type commanders in absolute agreement, and it went right into the plans from then on. Deyo, I guess, was DesLant then, Mort Deyo.[*] This would have been late summer and early autumn of '43, when all the ships were getting PPI, plan position indicator.[†]

Paul Stillwell: Just to go back some, do you have any other recollections of that tour that wound up being enjoyable when you were a Naval Academy duty officer in the late '30s?[‡]

---

[*] Rear Admiral Morton L. Deyo, USN, commanded Destroyer Force Atlantic Fleet from 14 December 1942 to 1 January 1944.
[†] Plan position indicator is a type of radar that presents essentially a geographical picture with one's own ship in the center of the scope and surrounding ships, planes, and land areas shown in their respective positions in terms of range and bearing. It was a vast improvement over the straight line radarscopes in use up to that time.
[‡] For more on this period, see the Naval Institute oral history of Rear Admiral Julian T. Burke, USN (Ret.), who graduated from the academy in the class of 1940. His oral history includes recollections of Wylie.

Admiral Wylie: Not really. Not really, except it was fun working with the kids, and I hadn't realized that that would be fun. Because I got niggled to death with two and three demerits and five demerits as a midshipman. I never put anybody on report for less than 20, and if it wasn't worth 20, I'd just speak to him, and very few of them. The only time in my life I've ever sat on the 50-yard line, going as a duty officer. It was fun working with the midshipmen. Joe Taussig was one of my midshipmen.[*] It was just fun. I enjoyed it.

Paul Stillwell: Who was superintendent then?

Admiral Wylie: I can't remember.

Paul Stillwell: Russell Willson was in 1941.[†]

Admiral Wylie: He may have been.

Paul Stillwell: I can't recall who preceded him.

Admiral Wylie: He had the niddy nods, didn't he, always going like that? I think so.

Paul Stillwell: Wilson Brown.[‡]

Admiral Wylie: Yes, he was the superintendent. I don't know much about him. He didn't impress me plus or minus.

Paul Stillwell: You got married in that period. Where had you met your wife?

---

[*] Midshipman Joseph K. Taussig, Jr., USN, graduated from the Naval Academy in the class of 1941 and subsequently earned a Navy Cross for his heroism while serving on board the battleship Nevada during the attack on Pearl Harbor later that year.
[†] Rear Admiral Russell Willson, USN, was superintendent of the Naval Academy from February 1941 to January 1942.
[‡] Rear Admiral Wilson Brown, USN, was superintendent from February 1938 to February 1941.

Admiral Wylie: When I came back from China. I got married about a year and a half after I came back, and then went out to San Diego in a newly commissioned destroyer. I commissioned four ships in the shipyard at Kearny which no longer exists: <u>Reid</u>, <u>Bristol</u>, <u>Fletcher</u>, and <u>Ault</u>—one as a junior man on board and one as the captain.[*]

Paul Stillwell: What are your recollections of Commander Carney putting the <u>Reid</u> in commission?[†]

Admiral Wylie: He's the only naval officer I know who I will admit is as good or better than I am at ship handling, and I've told him so. He was a marvelous captain, quite apart from ship handling.

Paul Stillwell: What about his leadership qualities?

Admiral Wylie: Superb. A little puffish sometimes. We went on a shakedown cruise. This would have been when, spring of '37? That was back when captains wrote their own itineraries for three-month shakedown, and ours was Mediterranean.

We left New York. I was the communications officer, and the gunnery officer, a lieutenant, and the chief engineer, lieutenant, were then both bachelors, as was I, but both of them were very heavily in the commodity market. They were gambling on cocoa. They kept pestering me for cocoa quotations, and I couldn't find them. You know, on the radio, you make the ship's newspaper. So after three or four days of this, I got bored with being pestered, so I made them up and ran the prices way up. The rules on sending personal messages, which were called Class E messages—maybe they still are—were pretty rigorous. They had to be important personal business.

Jesse Livermore was the great speculator of the '30s.[‡] He was well known and

---

[*] Federal Shipbuilding and Drydock Company, Kearny, New Jersey. Julian Burke's oral history also includes mention of an encounter when Wylie was executive officer of the <u>Bristol</u> (DD-453), which went into commission on 21 October 1941.

[†] USS <u>Reid</u> (DD-369), a <u>Mahan</u>-class destroyer, was commissioned 2 November 1936. She had a standard displacement of 1,480 tons, was 341 feet long, and 35 feet in the beam. Her design speed was 35 knots. She was armed with five 5-inch guns and twelve 21-inch torpedo tubes. She was eventually sunk by Japanese kamikaze aircraft attacks while operating in the Philippines on 11 December 1944.

[‡] See Richard Smitten, <u>Jesse Livermore: The World's Greatest Stock Trader</u> (Wiley, John & Sons, 2001).

frequently in the newspaper. So before we got to Gibraltar, I had the Securities Exchange Commission arrest Jesse Livermore and look for two unidentified naval officers, because the cocoa prices had simply gone through the roof. Then I got scared, and I told Captain Carney what I had been doing. So he fixed it so that when we stopped for fuel in Gibraltar, neither the engineer nor the gunner could go ashore, and then I gradually brought the stock price back. They finally got ashore in Bizerte and found a newspaper, and, of course, they were livid. I'd scared the hell out of them. I'd had the SEC after them, and I'd wiped them out between Gibraltar and Bizerte. I'd dropped the bottom out of the market. They were both going to get me, and Captain Carney stepped up. This is at the wardroom table, you see. He said, "Now, wait a minute, kids. It was I who didn't let you ashore." And that quieted the whole thing down. He enjoyed it hugely.

Paul Stillwell: I can just tell by the letters he sends to Shipmate that he has quite a sense of humor.*

Admiral Wylie: He's a marvel, but he's a cracking good naval officer.

Paul Stillwell: What else do you remember about him from that time in the ship?

Admiral Wylie: No specifics. He jumped on this cocoa futures bit with both feet, and it was he who decided to wipe them out between Gibraltar and Bizerte.

Paul Stillwell: I suppose you were getting much more of a chance to stand deck watches in there, really, than in the Augusta.

Admiral Wylie: Yes. We all stood watches. Everybody stood a watch except the exec. We made a watch in five. It wasn't bad. I think we had a total of seven officers, which was ample under the circumstances. It later carried twice that. We all stood deck watches.

---

* Shipmate is the monthly magazine published by the Naval Academy Alumni Association. Admiral Robert B. Carney, USN (Ret.), died 25 June 1990 at the age of 95.

Paul Stillwell: She was one of the gold-platers.*

Admiral Wylie: That's right.

Paul Stillwell: How did they compare with the four-stackers?

Admiral Wylie: Oh, my God! They were a different world. That's why I hated that four-piper so; it was a filthy, dirty old crock. I put it in the letter to my grandson. I didn't have any breakdowns in the first one, but I remember the day I went aboard her. I had a week in the hospital at Noumea and went aboard and relieved—the guy's name begins with A.† I was sitting in the wardroom on the port-side transom.

Paul Stillwell: This is in the Trever

Admiral Wylie: In the Trever. The captain's cabin in those four-pipers was off the wardroom, on the starboard side aft of the wardroom. That's how you got to it. I looked up in horror—the voice pipe running across over on that side was a big rat walking along the top of the voice pipe. The chief engineer was sitting beside me, and he whipped out a pistol and killed him. It was an air pistol. They all carried them. So the next day I finally got everybody off the ship and fumigated it. It was dreadful.

We had another funny—about that time, a little after that, say February, we began to get beer. The oilers started carrying beer. Of course, this was against the rules. I decided, all right, the next time we fuel, I'll take beer. I published the rules. I sent a young ensign in Noumea over—the logistic situation in SoPac was incredible.‡ There was a million, million, million dollars' worth of stores piled up on the beach there that nobody knew what was there. Anyway, I gave this guy a bottle of whiskey and told him

---

* The first of the "gold-platers," the modern destroyers designed in the 1930s, was the USS Farragut (DD-348), which had been commissioned 18 June 1934. They replaced the old four-pipers as the front-line destroyers in the U.S. Fleet.
† Lieutenant Wylie relieved Lieutenant Commander Dwight M. Agnew, USN, as commanding officer of the Trever on 6 February 1943.
‡ Noumea, New Caledonia, was the headquarters for Commander South Pacific Area and Force. Vice Admiral/Admiral William F. Halsey Jr., USN, served as Commander South Pacific Area (ComSoPac) from 18 October 1942 to 15 June 1944. He was promoted to four-star rank in November 1942.

to go over and get an icebox, which he did. It was, I guess 12 or 14 cubic foot. We painted it gray, bolted it to the after deckhouse. The rules were very clear. Anybody that wanted could have all the beer they wanted when we were, let us say, under the mango trees. They could either take the whaleboat, or which we had one, or a rubber boat, any party of them, go ashore, all the beer they wanted, but they could not drink when we were under way. One day the exec came up, and this was very odd, said, "The chief boatswain's mate would like to speak to you." This was highly formal. He had a jacket on, so you know it was formal.

He said, "Sir, we don't know who did it, but 17 bottles of beer are missing." That's all he said.

So I said, "All right. We published the rules, and next time we fuel, it goes back to the oiler." So it did.

About a week or ten days later, the exec said, "The chief boatswain's mate has another message for you."

He came up, and again he was very formal. He must have rehearsed it. He said, "Sir, we ain't never found out who did it, but he ain't going to do it again. Can we have the beer back?" So he'd beaten the hell out of somebody, obviously. So we got the beer back and never had any more trouble.

Paul Stillwell: A paternalistic system.

Admiral Wylie: Yes. "Sir, we ain't never found out who did it, but he ain't going to do it again. Can we have the beer back?"

Paul Stillwell: All in one breath, probably.

Admiral Wylie: Yes. That's just the way it came out. We never had any trouble after that.

Paul Stillwell: Where did the Reid go after her shakedown?

Admiral Wylie: West Coast, San Diego. I was in her for a year, then went to the destroyer tender Altair for a year.* I know Altair is no longer in commission. She was a World War I destroyer tender, merchant ship conversion, very low power, wide open nine knots. Whenever we had a fleet exercise that Altair went on, she was always made the fleet guide because she could only make nine knots. So she just steamed wide open all the time. One time we must have been going downwind, because the signal was framed later in the captain's cabin—came over from the commander in chief: "Altair slow down!"

But the system then was that junior officers had seven years at sea before their first shore duty. If possible, the seventh year was in something like a destroyer tender. So that was my seventh year at sea before I came ashore.

Paul Stillwell: What was the purpose of the seventh year being something like a destroyer tender?

Admiral Wylie: By that time people were getting married, and the tenders didn't go to sea as much as the others, and they'd already had six years all over the lot, you know. By then, presumably, they're old enough to do something useful in the tender, like in the repair department or something.

Paul Stillwell: What was your job in Altair?

Admiral Wylie: I don't remember. Maybe communications. I don't know.

Paul Stillwell: Did you still have mostly the old destroyers to service?

Admiral Wylie: By then we had a pretty fair sprinkling, about three or four squadrons of the gold-platers in San Diego. The old destroyers, by that time, were just about all laid

---

* Laid down as the steel-hulled freighter Edisto on 18 December 1918, the ship was delivered to the Navy on 5 December 1921, classified as a destroyer tender, AD-11, and renamed Altair. She served the Navy for the next 25 years, through World War II, before being decommissioned 21 June 1946. She was transferred to the Maritime Commission and subsequently scrapped.

up in San Diego. There must have been 50 of them in the back channel. I don't know whether anybody told you this or not, but there were a few old destroyers still in commission, but they had gradually accumulated in the back channel. Of course, by that time spare parts for World War I destroyers were very hard to come by. This is secondhand. I don't vouch for it. When they recommissioned those ships, there was a standard up-and-down pump, a reciprocating pump, that may have been makeup feed or something, you know. The crankshaft for this one-cylinder, up-and-down pump was exactly the size of a swab handle. The original shafts were brittle and broke. Every single destroyer in the back channel, when you scraped the grease off it, had a swab handle—enough said?—for the piston rod.

Paul Stillwell: Some of those probably were ships that went over to the British.[*]

Admiral Wylie: Well, they must have put in an emergency order for a lot of makeup feed pump piston rods. Yes, they were pretty bad midnight scavengers.

Paul Stillwell: Anything else you remember about the Altair

Admiral Wylie: No. I sailed under Captain Craven, whom I loved, Francis Craven. Really not a notable year—I mean, professionally.[†]

Paul Stillwell: You've talked about the Naval Academy. Then you went to the Bristol, another new ship.[‡]

Admiral Wylie: How do you know all this?

---

[*] In September 1940 President Franklin D. Roosevelt concluded a deal with Prime Minister Winston Churchill of Great Britain whereby the United States transferred 50 destroyers to the Royal Navy for use against German submarines. In return the United States received 99-year leases to British bases in the West Indies, Bermuda, and Newfoundland.
[†] Commander Francis S. Craven, USN.
[‡] USS Bristol (DD-453), a Gleaves-class destroyer, was commissioned 21 October 1941. She had a standard displacement of 1,630 tons, was 348 feet long, and 36 feet in the beam. Her top speed was 35 knots. She was armed with five 5-inch guns and five 21-inch torpedo tubes. She was later torpedoed and sunk on 13 October 1943 while escorting a convoy in the Mediterranean.

Paul Stillwell: I've got it right here.

Admiral Wylie: Oh, for heaven's sake. Yes. Under Chester Wood.* She was commissioned in 1941 and almost immediately started convoying in the North Atlantic, which was not publicly admitted. Until December 7, we never went all the way. Again, I've got it in a letter to my grandson. The destination was MOMP. Have you ever heard of MOMP?

Paul Stillwell: Mid-ocean meeting point.

Admiral Wylie: That's where we turned over.† After the seventh of December, we went on to Londonderry, the North Atlantic. You know the Plimsoll Mark.‡ The lowest mark is WNA, Winter North Atlantic.§ There's a very good reason for that. That's a rough ocean, that western ocean.

Paul Stillwell: What do you recall about those operations—any specific incidents?

Admiral Wylie: It was heartbreaking to have a ship torpedoed. I don't think we ever got any submarines. We dropped a lot of depth charges, but no reason then or now to think we actually caught a submarine.

A couple of nice anecdotes, again, which are in that typed stuff, wherever it is. The most delightful one is the Saint-Pierre-Miquelon bit. We got to Londonderry one time, and I heard this in a bar from an RN guy. I can't vouch for it. I have written but have not had an answer from the historical section at Greenwich, because I've got it as a

---

* Lieutenant Commander Chester C. Wood, USN, was the first commanding officer when the Bristol was commissioned.
† Because of neutrality laws then in effect, U.S. Navy ships were not permitted to escort convoys all the way to the British Isles. They turned them over in mid-ocean to British escort ships for the rest of the trip.
‡ The Plimsoll Mark is a load-line marking painted on the side of a merchant ship's hull. It shows where the waterline should be under various sea conditions and thus how much cargo a ship can carry safely. The name honors Samuel Plimsoll (1824-1898), a British ship owner who instituted the load-line markings on his ships.
§ The lowest mark would result in the greatest amount of freeboard, that is, the distance between the waterline and the top deck.

footnote in a manuscript, which the Proceedings is now evaluating, by the way, book manuscript. I think they'll probably turn it down, but, anyway, there was a French corvette—this was a real mixed bag—Canadian corvette, U.S. destroyer, senior officer, Canadian corvette, probably British corvette, maybe two Canadians, a Pole and a Free Frenchman.

When the Frenchman got—this is how the story goes, and I haven't confirmed it yet—to Londonderry, he very proudly presented two prisoners to the British. They were the governor and his wife from Saint-Pierre-Miquelon. This was the Gaullist Free French corvette, British-built, French-manned. For some inscrutable reason, the British would not accept them, and told them to take them back. This is the story of the "Lady and the Tiger," because as soon as the governor was taken by the corvette, Saint-Pierre-Miquelon became Free French, Gaullist. What the hell happened to them? "The Lady and the Tiger?"

The Pole was another case. I was surprised to find a Polish corvette in the North Atlantic, and I asked in Londonderry. They had perhaps half a dozen corvettes manned by Polish officers and men, and they worked normally the North Sea. What had happened, as I got the story—again, secondhand—they had come upon a downed German airplane with a couple of men still clinging to the wreckage and shot them in the water. When they got back to port, the British reproved them and said, "We don't do that. You never shoot people without sentence of a court-martial. So the Poles went out again, came on another German downed plane, hauled the survivors on board, held a court-martial, shot them, and threw them back. So their penalty was two round trips in the North Atlantic. That's why they were with us. You have no idea of the bitterness.

Mrs. Wylie stayed with her parents in New Jersey during the war, and they had a Polish maid. I got home occasionally, maybe once a year. The first question that was asked me by Josie, "How many Germans you kill?" Bitter, deep bitter.

Paul Stillwell: Poland had been invaded, and Britain hadn't.

Admiral Wylie: Yes.

Paul Stillwell: Any especially memorable storms you were in on this patrol?

Admiral Wylie: No. I've only been in about two or three hurricanes, and oddly enough, they were in the early '50s, and I was in the amphibious force. The North Atlantic may as well be a hurricane all the time. I was in the Pacific hurricanes. During the Okinawa bit, I broke off from the worst of them. I left the formation, because I thought it was being so dreadfully ill managed. Again, I have written that to my grandson, the particular incident in there, and I won't kill your time with it. As I say, one of those I've written on it, you can keep if you want it. The other one, if you'd send it back, I'd appreciate it. You've got a better Xerox machine than I have.

Paul Stillwell: Did you get into Iceland at all?

Admiral Wylie: Offshore, never into harbor.

Paul Stillwell: Did you have any liberty ports?

Admiral Wylie: No, we worked out of Portland, which is by far the most convenient U.S. port for the North Atlantic.* I don't know why they've never based any ships there. They did during the war; battleships were in there, as well as destroyers.

Paul Stillwell: I talked to Admiral McCrea, who was the first skipper of the Iowa, and he didn't get his rudder over in time, the second turn.†

Admiral Wylie: There's a big rock.

Paul Stillwell: He creased the underwater hull of the Iowa.

---

* This is Portland, Maine, on Casco Bay.
† On 16 July 1943, while completing a transit from New York City, the Iowa cut a long gash in her bottom while entering Casco Bay, Maine, shortly after low water. The commanding officer at the time was Captain John L. McCrea, USN. McCrea, who retired as a vice admiral, discussed the incident in his Naval Institute oral history.

Admiral Wylie: I didn't know that, but there's an ugly rock eight smack in the middle of the entrance once you get inside. Yes, that's a good port to work out of.

Paul Stillwell: How many days at a time would you go out?

Admiral Wylie: A slow convoy, six or seven knots, a couple of weeks, I guess, maybe two or three weeks. Everything battered, gun mount facings mashed in, this sort of thing, but manageable.

Paul Stillwell: Did you talk to the crews of the merchant ships at all? How willing were they to undertake this tour?

Admiral Wylie: I can't answer that. We picked up a lot of them, but I didn't talk to them much. The only amusing one that comes to mind, maybe a day out of Portland, we came upon a lifeboat, and the master was in it with maybe eight or ten other men. I had him up to lunch and asked him if he'd lost all his cargo. He said, "Most of it." But he said, "The important stuff I saved."

I said, "How did you save it?"

Around his neck he had three or four what could have been leather bags of industrial diamonds.

Paul Stillwell: Gee.

Admiral Wylie: Fat bags, baseball size. That was the important part of his cargo. The rest of it was probably almost as valuable. It was mica from India. I don't know what we use mica for, but it was critical, whatever it was. He lost that, but he saved the industrial diamonds. They were on a string around his neck—I think three, four, five bags, probably four. I picked up over 1,000 people during the war, one way or another, 100 of them carrier aviators. I didn't keep exact records, but I remember going over 100 carrier aviators. Seven hundred of them I got off <u>Northampton</u> with Bill Cole; he was my skipper, and I was exec.* I wrote that up, too, for my grandson, so I won't bore you with that. During the war, over 1,000 people.

Paul Stillwell: Did you develop any special techniques for pulling people out of the water, since they were likely to be tired?

Admiral Wylie: Sure did. We got down to two things. One carrier—I'll come to the aviators next. But when we finally got down to the South Pacific and got the flavor of the place, my captain and I, we knew that if we survived we'd probably have to rescue some people whose ships sank. So, obviously, he was the captain, he'd stay on the bridge. I took 200-fathom shots of 21-thread line and tied off pieces of life jacket to it. We kept it stored aft. We had one whaleboat.

When we got the Northampton people is a good illustration. We backed in. All these men were in filthy, oily water. We put the boat in the water, and the boat would take one end of this—500-600 feet—make as big a circle as he could, and come back to the fantail with strict orders that he was not to pick up anyone who wasn't in immediate danger of drowning. So then we had two ends of this, and we started hauling in one end while he took the other line and made a big loop around the other quarter. We had cargo nets over the side, and we rigged a jigger back there with a wire stretcher in case somebody couldn't climb the cargo nets. We got over 700 men, and I think Drayton was the other ship.† She got 75 or something. So it worked.

Now, as far as aviators go, in the last year of the war I had the flotilla commander embarked, the senior squadron. We had three squadrons in the circular screen—18 to 24—give or take. But my commodore, since he was the flotilla commander, I never got picket duty, you know, go out 50 miles. That's where people got hurt. So I took all the night plane-guard duty, and by that time the CVLs—each of the carrier task groups had a CVL with them, a cruiser conversion, and they had embarked the first of the night air

---

* The heavy cruiser Northampton (CA-26) sank as a result of being torpedoed during the Battle of Tassafaronga, near Guadalcanal, early on the morning of 1 December 1942. Wylie was then executive officer of the destroyer Fletcher; Commander William M. Cole, USN, was the commanding officer.
† This rescue is described on page 209 of Theodore Roscoe, United States Destroyer Operations in World War II (Annapolis: U.S. Naval Institute, 1953). The book credits the Fletcher with rescuing 600 survivors and the Drayton (DD-366) with 128.

groups—fighters, bombers, torpedo planes.* They only flew at night. So I took all the night plane-guard duty, and that's where I got most of my 100 aviators, not all by any means.

Our system was very easy. The first thing is you get on the landing frequency so you can tell who's going to have an accident, and very often you can, either from a specific report from a defect or from tension in the voice. Ride up real close on the starboard quarter, a little closer than the daytime guide, but way out so your mast wasn't going to confuse him. Run two lines, three lines up from the waist of the ship where you have a cargo net ready to go over, and a jigger with a wire stretcher, if you're going to need it, outside the lifelines to the forecastle. And on each side you've got a swimmer, and he's got a harness on, one of the lines to the harness, and he carries one other line with him, or something, maybe two. So when you get up, you scoot under the stern of the carrier, and you pull right rudder and start backing down, because they usually go over the port bow. But it works if a guy makes a water landing outside the formation. Lay the bow as close alongside as you can.

The first thing that goes over is an outsized monkey fist that will float.† Heave it straight to him as you can with the line. The swimmer goes over, he goes out, and he takes a snap hook and takes it around this guy under his shoulders, you know. Then all these lines are hauled in to the waist of the ship, which is the lowest point. The first thing we found out was that they couldn't climb up, because no aviator will let go of a parachute under any circumstances. So we had to have a boatswain in the water or a seaman with a very sharp knife. As the guy started up the cargo net, he'd cut the webbing straps. Then the guy could climb up, because he didn't have this million pounds on his back, this waterlogged parachute. He'd get up on deck, and there would be—almost always it was exactly the same pattern, "Oh, gee, thanks, guys. Who in the hell stole my parachute?" And then you'd give it to him, and he'd look sheepish and give it to the nearest seaman.

---

* A plane-guard destroyer steams astern—or off on one quarter—of an aircraft carrier in order to recover aircraft crew members who go into the water. The Independence (CVL-22)-class light carriers were built on cruiser hulls. Each had a standard displacement of 10,662 tons; full-load, 14,751 tons; length, 622 feet; beam, 72 feet, maximum width 109 feet, top speed of 31.6 knots; and capability of handling about 30 aircraft.

† A monkey fist is a weighted knot tied at the end of the heaving line to give it some heft and carry when thrown from a ship.

But, yes, that system of going up with a swimmer on the forecastle and lines leading back to the waist, for me it worked. As far as I know, if a guy got out of his airplane, I got every one of them that got out. They didn't all get out.

Paul Stillwell: Was there a difference in working with the CVL, as opposed to a CV?

Admiral Wylie: No, not really. They were all straight decks, no angled decks then. A CVL was vastly more vulnerable. My commodore and I, we developed a great fondness—I don't even remember the name of it; it might have been the Cabot, I don't remember—but we'd always keep the screen oriented so that we in Ault, my ship, were right outboard. Now, he didn't have anything but 40-millimeter guns. So when we closed in tight for daytime air defense, I always got in 100 feet outboard of Cabot, because it made them feel good to have our six 5-inch guns. And if there had been a torpedo loose, it might have got us instead of Cabot, you know, and the cost is less. But we developed a very close relationship with those guys. You know, I can't remember the name of it today.*

Paul Stillwell: Who was the commodore you were carrying?

Admiral Wylie: John Higgins, absolutely marvelous.† He never came on my bridge without asking permission. Can you imagine it? I never could break him of that habit. And he didn't have a bridge; this was his bridge too. But he always asked permission. We got along real good. He wasn't supposed to be in my ship. His assigned flagship, I think, was English. I was the third one out of Kearny in this consecutive shakedown, which was a rarity to go to Bermuda for a shakedown, you know, whatever that outfit is that measures how good you are.

Paul Stillwell: COTCLant or something.

---

* During the Okinawa operation in the spring of 1945 the destroyer Ault operated as part of Task Group 58.3, which included the large carriers Essex (CV-9), Bunker Hill (CV-17), and Hancock (CV-19) and the light carriers Cabot (CVL-28) and Bataan (CVL-29).
† Captain John M. Higgins, Commander Destroyer Squadron 62. Later, as a rear admiral, Higgins commanded forces in the Korean War.

Admiral Wylie: Something.

Paul Stillwell: Operational Training Command.

Admiral Wylie: Whatever it was. Anyway, you owed them a week in Bermuda when you first got commissioned. Because I was in the fourth ship I'd commissioned out of Kearny, all the yard workmen who had been peons when I first went there were the foremen, so I could get anything I wanted, much to the dismay and annoyance of the superintendent of shipbuilding. For instance, voice pipes. Voice pipes never worked. They were all at right angles all over the lot. I didn't have a single voice pipe that had a curvature of less than a 3-foot radius. The result was that there was perfect clarity one end to the other. Little things like that.

Commodore came aboard, and he saw all my little goodies, and he never left, you know. It was just better than the other ships. We had a little walkway around part of the bridge, and there was a compass out there, and there was a rudder-angle indicator, and there were other things, you know, repeaters for the engine-order telegraph. Well, I got with the foreman one day, and we drew a picture of it. You could stand at either pelorus and see every instrument on the forward part of the bridge, which you couldn't see in the pilothouse, because they built me a slightly curved mounting board so that the angle from one pelorus to the other pelorus was the same on both sides.[*] You see the same thing today in a BMW. They've got the curved instrument panel. We had that. We had that sort of goodies that really don't cost much more but drive superintendents of shipbuilding crazy because they're different.[†] The commodore never left.

Paul Stillwell: Where did you put all those people from the Northampton when you managed to get them aboard?

---

[*] A pelorus is a combination of a compass repeater and stand, usually mounted on the wing of a ship's bridge in a place that has a wide arc of vision. The compass is usually about chest high to facilitate the use of a bearing circle or alidade to take azimuth bearings on other ships or on objects ashore.
[†] The supervisor of shipbuilding is a naval officer who is the Navy's on-scene representative to monitor the progress of construction and repair of Navy ships at commercial shipyards.

Admiral Wylie: We had to keep most of them below decks, bring them up in relays. Of course, they came aboard absolutely filthy with grease, and the clothing went over the side as fast as we could get rid of it, and get them hosed down. Everybody in the ship's company surrendered all the clothes they had to these guys. The cooks turned to. The galley was just running for the next 48 hours until we got back, I think, to Espiritu, or wherever it was, their cooks and ours cooking steadily. Everybody heaved around. We kept a limit on the number of people topside, and somehow the exec or the boatswain or somebody arranged for people to come up in relays to get some fresh air. Yes, we had a stability problem.

Paul Stillwell: What do you remember about putting the Fletcher in commission? You described the others there at Kearny, and that was a special ship, the first of a class.

Admiral Wylie: That was strange. They hadn't organized the training commands. What did you call it, COTCLant or something?

Paul Stillwell: Yes.

Admiral Wylie: They hadn't organized those, and our shakedown was to the Caribbean and back—escorting convoys, losing ships. I mean, merchantmen. I don't think we caught any with our depth charges. Where did we go? Probably San Juan. I don't remember. So that was our shakedown. We went down as far as Trinidad. That was when we were on our way west. Chinese telegraph. For reasons not known to me, it was supposed to be super ultra secret that we were going to the Pacific, and Bill Cole said, "We can't keep that quiet. See what you can do." So while we were in Brooklyn, before we left, I made sure we had a worldwide portfolio of charts, but I twice sent the quartermaster over to whatever street it is in New York where the district headquarters was to be sure we had every single chart available for the Persian Gulf.

Paul Stillwell: Ninety Church Street.

Admiral Wylie: Ninety Church Street. The Persian Gulf. So we went on down and went to Trinidad, took a convoy from Trinidad over to the Caribbean side of the canal, and the ship's company still thought we were going to the Persian Gulf. So we didn't say anything. Everything that had to be done ashore we did on the Atlantic side. Then we started through the canal, and you've never seen such a stunned, surprised ship's company in your life. Because we'd done all our business on the Atlantic end, we didn't even stop. We just kept going on the Pacific side. Refueled in the Atlantic—O'Bannon, Fletcher, and company—and I think we steamed 4,500 miles on one kettle at 13 knots till we got to Bora Bora. There was an oiler in the harbor there, a commercial harbor for fuel. We were down around 10%.

Paul Stillwell: You had to go that slow, too, to conserve fuel.

Admiral Wylie: Yes, 13 knots. I think that's where the point on the curve was for most efficient steaming, and one kettle. We were both pretty close to 10% when we got into Bora Bora.

Paul Stillwell: What do you remember about her time in the shipyard as she was being finished up?

Admiral Wylie: Nothing.

Paul Stillwell: I wonder if she had any special InSurv or something because she was first of the class?*

Admiral Wylie: The only oddity I remember—when we were commissioned, of course, we set a watch, and there was a watch aft, he was armed, there was a watch forward. The first lieutenant had the duty the first night we were in commission. He made his rounds of the ship. He went up on the forecastle; the forecastle watch was sitting on the bitts, and his rifle was lying on the deck. The first lieutenant ate him up one side and down

---

* InSurv—the Board of Inspection and Survey.

another. Remember at that time sentries used to wear a board on their belt with their orders on it, which they did, carried their orders right here. With a great dramatic flourish, young Tom, the first lieutenant, pointed at the board and said, "Goddamn it, can't you read?"

The man sad, "No, sir." We had three illiterates aboard. We didn't know that. But that's the only thing I remember about fitting out, except that the Brooklyn yard did a good job. I mean, they were very fast and efficient. I think I remember Iowa being on the ways there. Wasn't Iowa built in Brooklyn?

Paul Stillwell: Yes.

Admiral Wylie: She may have been launched or something about that time.*

Paul Stillwell: She was commissioned on Washington's Birthday in '43.

Admiral Wylie: I'm foggy. Identity's unclear.

Paul Stillwell: Could you discuss, please, the thing that we talked about before the tape recorder was running, about the problems with the torpedoes and so forth?

Admiral Wylie: My position on this is very simple: every officer that's ever had anything to do with torpedoes should be court-martialed. And if he really isn't guilty, he'll be acquitted. The torpedoes—of course, the magnetic impulse exploders simply didn't work. We found that out early enough to set them to run at the least depth, which is six or eight feet. They actually ran eight or ten feet below that. So our contact explosions were very rare, and the contact exploders didn't go off. I've unloaded 20 torpedoes in anger. I know some of them hit. This is infuriating. The smokeless powder wasn't smokeless; the flashless powder wasn't flashless. Now, the flashless powder we cured by taking the 5-inch cases apart and putting in every one of them, under the cork, a

---

* The Iowa was launched 27 August 1942 at the New York Navy Yard, about the time the Fletcher was leaving for the Pacific.

piece of cigarette package tinfoil. Everybody had to save it after somebody found out. So as soon as we'd get new ammunition aboard, the gunner's mates would take all the 5-inch cartridges apart, put a piece of cigarette package tinfoil in every one of them, and then it was flashless.

Paul Stillwell: What was the magic trick there?

Admiral Wylie: I don't know. I don't know. Whatever it did, it did. Smokeless powder was dreadful. It was so dirty, it always started fires if it got into the whaleboat or something, you know.

The Navy had its own automatic weapons at the beginning of the war. They were a .50-caliber machine gun and a 1.1-inch machine gun. Each of them had more moving parts—and moving parts not parallel to the bore—than any other gun that's ever been conceived, and they were always broken. Finally, somebody must have gotten too exasperated with the Bureau of Ordnance and made them buy the Oerlikon 20-millimeter and the Bofors 40-millimeter, and they were superb. Well, you know about the stuff that didn't explode or ran. The depth charges—we had cylinders with unpredictable sinking rate until somebody saw the British with a teardrop that you could predict the sinking rate on for depth-charging. I don't know about the mines. But we just had dreadful ordnance. The torpedoes, of course, were the worst, simply because it cost so many people so much risk to unload one of them, particularly the submarines. But they were dreadful.

Paul Stillwell: What was the answer you got when you went to OpNav and inquired about these?

Admiral Wylie: There was an electric torpedo. I don't know whether it ever came into service. It was not for destroyers. It might have been for submarines; I cannot answer. But it was developed by the mine section, not the torpedo section, of BuOrd.[*] They just were excluded.

---

[*] BuOrd—Bureau of Ordnance.

Paul Stillwell: They wouldn't let the torpedo people work on them.

Admiral Wylie: They wouldn't let them tinker with it, because they'd bitch it up.

Paul Stillwell: Do you want to try again tomorrow or the next day?

Admiral Wylie: Sure, sure. Afternoon.

Interview Number 1 with Rear Admiral Joseph C. Wylie, Jr., U.S. Navy (Retired)

Place: Admiral Wylie's home, Portsmouth, Rhode Island

Date: Wednesday, 22 May 1985

Interviewer: Paul Stillwell

Paul Stillwell: Admiral, to begin this day's discussion, I wonder if you could provide your views on what the value is of having a navy.

Admiral Wylie: What we're talking about are the flexibility and employability of naval forces, as contrasted to land-based forces, both soldiery and air. I had nothing to do with this one. I don't remember where I was at the time, but you may recall that during Mr. Eisenhower's presidency, Mr. Nixon went to South America, and there were great demonstrations against him in a number of places.

Paul Stillwell: I think Venezuela.

Admiral Wylie: Venezuela was probably the worst.* What nobody knows is that while he was in Venezuela—I'll show you that later—there was a carrier offshore with helicopters, then quite new. The embassy roof would not take a helicopter, but there was an easy access to the building next door to the embassy, and the whole time he was having trouble in Venezuela, there were naval forces with helicopters standing by to go in and snatch him out. Nobody knew they were there. That's probably the most minor one of the four or five here.

About 1964, the Santo Domingo affair. I was then the two-star working flag officer, the junior, on Admiral Page Smith's CinCLantFlt staff, and we had just really got organized with the opcon center at Norfolk.† This is probably a super-deluxe apparatus now. Then it was in a new building, but it was fairly primitive. When it came time to

---

* In Caracas, Venezuela, on 13 May 1958, three windows of the limousine in which Vice President Richard Nixon was riding were smashed by rocks, and both he and Mrs. Nixon were spat upon. A Navy task force was about 30 miles off the coast of Venezuela in the event it was needed to protect Nixon. However, he decided to cancel the rest of his planned appearances there and flew to Puerto Rico on 14 May.

† Admiral Harold Page Smith, USN, served as Supreme Allied Commander Atlantic, Commander in Chief Atlantic, and Commander in Chief Atlantic Fleet from 30 April 1963 to 30 April 1965. Opcon—operational control.

staff it, of course, we had difficulties with BuPers, so I went up there.* And at that time there was a plethora of good three-stripe aviators who had had such limited duty that they were essentially not going to be promoted, and they knew it. But they were cracking good officers. So I got half a dozen of them for the watch officers in the CinCLantFlt opcon center. And that's the kind of work that, when they hadn't been in a cockpit, they'd been doing all their lives in the control, so, you know, they were good.

One Saturday afternoon—you'll have to look up the dates; I don't remember—there came a message from the U.S. embassy in Santo Domingo. The ambassador was in Georgia. This was his number two, Mr. Reid Cabral, who was one of the governing triumvirate.† He had come to the embassy in a panic, saying there was a coup brewing. So they telephoned. I lived on the compound there. I walked over, and within an hour, we had to cancel my last message. No crisis. It was Saturday, and things were dull, so I talked to the watch over and said, "Look, let's make believe," because it smelled fishy. "Make believe there is a coup. What can we do? What should we do? Where haven't we got our homework done?" Etc., etc., etc.

And, of course, one of the things in a situation like that is that it protects your extraction of U.S. and what we called—really with a straight face—friendly foreign nationals. These are the foreign nationals to whom we're indebted, so on and so forth. So they spent all that night getting checked out, working with the State Department. As it later turned out, we had everybody in the Dominican Republic taken, except the University of Michigan band, which was playing at a hotel down west of the city. We had all the rest of them.

Sunday morning, I would guess 9:00 o'clock, there came another message, and it looked bleak. It looked like maybe this coup was really on track. Nothing definitive but worth a gamble. Admiral Smith was out on the golf course, and I telephoned him and said, "I want to move your forces, Admiral."

He said, "Go ahead." He knew what I was talking about.

---

* BuPers—Bureau of Naval Personnel.
† The Army-backed civilian triumvirate that governed the nation was led by Donald Reid Cabral.

I telephoned Howard Caldwell, who was the commandant of the naval district in San Juan.* In addition to the coded messages, I said, "I can't tell you much, Howard, but get them under way. Keep one ship back to pick up stragglers. Move them over, in effect, 20 miles offshore of Santo Domingo," about a day's run. He's a marvelous man, and he neither argued nor asked questions. You don't get a phone call like that as a joke.

So then came Monday, and it blew. The coup occurred. At the 8:00 o'clock conference, of course, the question was, "What are we going to do?" These were amphibious ships that had part of a Marine battalion embarked. A lot of more or less empty amphibious ships, as well as those with embarked Marines. The question was, "What are we to do?"

Admiral Smith was very direct. He said, "Don't do anything. By 10:30 your opposite numbers in Washington will begin to phone you, and they will ask, 'Where's the fleet?' And your answer will be, 'Twenty miles offshore. What are our orders?'" And it worked.†

What I'm illustrating, of course, is the flexibility and the capacity to do something on the basis of hints and cues that would never pass a formal inspection. See, we started these guys 24 hours early. It was a 24-hour run. And it worked. Of course, from Monday morning on, everybody and his brother had to get into the act. Marines—they wouldn't stay out of it. Of course, they wanted to get in. The Army—one of the two airborne divisions was in the act. The best performance was laid on by the Tactical Air Command, who had an agency, a headquarters of some sort, up one of the peninsulas from Norfolk. Where did NASA used to be? Somewhere down in the lower peninsulas of Virginia. You know where I'm talking about?

Paul Stillwell: Langley?

---

* Rear Admiral Henry Howard Caldwell, USN, served as Commandant of the Tenth Naval District from February 1963 to September 1965.
† Leftists in the Dominican Republic rebelled against the established government on 24 April 1965. On 28 April U.S. President Lyndon Johnson dispatched a 405-man expeditionary brigade to that nation. They landed by helicopter that day to protect the lives and property of American citizens caught in the revolt. By 29 April, 1,600 Marines had landed, and by 7 May 6,000 Marines were ashore and another 2,000 offshore. They were followed by Army troops, bringing the U.S. combat presence by 11 May to more than 11,000 troops. Navy ships evacuated more than 4,300 civilians during the operation.

Admiral Wylie: Yes, Langley. They were simply superb. I was working with a young brigadier over there, just one of the most able men I've ever worked with blind. We'd never seen each other, of course. All that thing went in. It's of interest to note that the only other question that Admiral Smith asked at that Monday morning conference was, "Where is Balaguer?" None of us knew who Balaguer was.[*] As it turned out, he was teaching at Columbia, and as it turned out, he was the guy that was finally taken down there to restore order in Santo Domingo. But old smarty over here, that was his first question: "Where's Balaguer?" We found out later that morning, but that's enough about that San to Domingo thing.

The airborne division, I forget which one it was, 101st or the other one, 82nd, was much better than the Marines.[†] The Air Force Tactical Air Command, who ran the airlifts, the air stream it was, was marvelous. I think the Marine Corps learned from that that it had been living a little bit on reputation, because after that they came up with a round turn.[‡] The 82nd—or 101st, whichever—was better organized, better led, and better managed in that situation. It was a damn good lesson for the Marine Corps.

Paul Stillwell: The Marines did put ashore a detachment that was embarked on <u>Newport News</u>. I'm not sure if it was on that occasion.

Admiral Wylie: I don't remember.

Paul Stillwell: In the Dominican Republic.

Admiral Wylie: Chief Masterson was the senior Navy flag officer down there.[§] I don't know where he wore his flag. I don't recall.

One funny—intelligence, as usual, as it was a year or two ago in Grenada, was

---

[*] Joaquin Balaguer had been president of the Dominican Republic from 1960 until his forced resignation in January 1962.
[†] Elements of the Army's 82nd Airborne Division participated in the Dominican Republic operation.
[‡] In nautical phraseology, taking a round turn means putting two loops of line over a bitt or bollard, thus restraining the ship at the end of the line. In a figurative sense it means restraining unwanted behavior.
[§] Vice Admiral Kleber S. Masterson, USN, commanded the Second Fleet from April 1964 to August 1966. His oral history is in the Naval Institute collection.

simply appalling.* The air landing site was a field outside Santo Domingo. What nobody knew was that it had been developed for poor people's housing. It was just covered with three-story houses. There was a field outside Santo Domingo, we found out from an Esso roadmap.† Somebody bungled one up. It was the best map we had. Chief Masterson and his flag lieutenant, whose name escapes me, went ashore. They went ashore, found the field dark. The flag lieutenant, who was an aviator, climbed up in the tower, turned the lights on, and talked the stream in until an air control apparatus arrived in one of the planes. But that's exactly what happened to those poor guys in Grenada. They had ten-year-old maps or something. They weren't up to date. The intelligence apparatus consistently failed us in timeliness.

Item—Nixon trip, Santo Domingo. The 1956 war, that was the one in which Britain and, I think, France, joined the Israelis in attacking the canal, because the Egyptians said they were going to nationalize it.‡ There had been an agreement, I guess in the aftermath of World War II, that the Allies—United States, Britain, France, et. al.— would not read each other's mail. By this I mean read their friends' radio transmissions. As far as I know, we're the only one of those countries that observed that. It was a dumb, dumb thing to do. And that's why we were caught short. We had absolutely no warning on that. I pray we're not making that same silly mistake now. What happened was, when that thing blew, everybody in Washington was caught by surprise, including the uniformed services. Most of the secretaries went a long ways away on trips. They just got out of town. The services all furied around—what can they do?

Admiral Burke was then the CNO.§ There really wasn't much anybody could do, except Burke and his Navy. What he did was take the Sixth Fleet, which was then in the western Med, and move it to the eastern Med. He took what was, in effect, the Second

---

* In October 1983 the United States mounted a joint-service operation to occupy Grenada in the Caribbean after a Marxist military coup overthrew the island's government. The overthrow and subsequent developments led to concern about the safety of approximately 1,000 U.S. citizens on the island.
† Esso was an oil company; it is now known as Exxon.
‡ On 26 July 1956 President Gamal Nasser of Egypt announced that his country was nationalizing the Suez Canal Company. Israeli forces invaded Egypt's Sinai Peninsula on 29 October 1956. Britain and France then intervened militarily on behalf of Israel in an unsuccessful attempt to secure the Suez Canal, which was damaged and closed to traffic. Rather than support the British and French, the United States asked for a United Nations resolution to end the fighting. A cease-fire took effect on 6 November.
§ Admiral Arleigh A. Burke, USN, served as Chief of Naval Operations from 17 August 1955 to 1 August 1961. His oral history is in the Naval Institute collection.

Fleet, out of Norfolk on the East Coast, and sent it to a dead spot between Madeira and the Azores, where there were no ocean traffic lanes. He took part of the Seventh Fleet, about half, sent it down through the Sunda Strait and over in the Indian Ocean and the Arabian Sea. He took the other half of the Seventh Fleet and moved it down to the South China Sea, that is, abreast the Philippines. He took the ships in Hawaii and sent them up off Japan. And he took the ships on the West Coast, mostly San Diego, Long Beach, San Pedro, and sent them out west of the Hawaiian Islands. In effect, he moved the whole United States Fleet around the world in two directions to close in on the Middle East. Nobody knew what for, but he just closed in.

There were several aspects of that that were interesting. One is, for the first time in a long while, the ships actually observed an absolute electronic silence, no transmissions. They could receive, but no transmissions. The result was that the Soviets went crazy. Two-thirds of our naval attachés around the world said they were being pestered by their Soviet opposite numbers to know what the United States Navy was doing, even in Indonesia.

Admiral Burke had on his desk a red telephone, which went to somebody in the White House. I don't know who it was. It was not Mr. Eisenhower. Maybe it was one of the military aides. I think Sherman Adams was probably still in business then, but I don't remember.[*] Anyway, it was somebody who had direct access to the President. He had a white telephone that went to somebody in the State Department. I think Mr. Dulles was then Secretary.[†] It may have been to him, I don't know. I was never in there when he talked on those phones. Presumably, they knew what was going on. Admiral Burke didn't bother to tell his colleagues in the Joint Chiefs; he just passed off.

While the Navy was doing all of this, the Air Force was absolutely air-bound, because they knew they dare not move any bombers, and they dare not move any fighters. The only thing they could do was to send them some tankers up to Thule in northern Greenland. That was the only place they could send even tankers without hitting headlines. The Army, about a year before, had gone through one of its periodic

---

[*] Sherman Adams, who had served in the Marine Corps in World War I, was governor of New Hampshire from January 1949 to January 1953. He served as assistant to President Dwight D. Eisenhower from 21 January 1953 until his resignation on 22 September 1958.
[†] John Foster Dulles served as Secretary of State from 21 January 1953 to 22 April 1959.

reorganizations and had an apparatus which they called the Strategic Army Corps, and this was their emergency crew, you know, ready forces. Of course, in the middle '50s, the Army was still flat on its back, recovering from that chaotic, disastrous demobilization of the prior decade. To jump ahead, the Army finally found the cooks and bakers for the Strategic Army Corps in Fort Hood, out in the state of Washington, about five weeks after this thing started.[*] They were just air-bound.

I think the thing broke in late October, nine or ten days before the election of 1956, which was, let us say, on the sixth of November, but about ten days before that.[†] During the whole while, the joint apparatus, the Joint Staff, was churning around, trying to develop a paper to send to the President to get his approval. Well, there really wasn't anything to go in that paper except what Burke had done with the fleet. That only got to the Joint Staff a couple of days before the election. The ships were all in place. They finally got that paper completed about the day before election. Mr. Eisenhower would not receive it until the polls had closed in the state of Washington on election day. It was delivered to him, and he nodded and initialed it, in the Wardman Park Hotel, in the victory celebration.

What I've gone into this somewhat longer than I expected recital is to illustrate to another generation, if they ever see these documents of yours, the enormous employability of forces at sea, as contrasted to land-based forces. We sometimes tend in our service to be too anxious to establish bases. Better that we not. That was also very interesting later. This was the period, and you may have gotten it in some of the other interviews, of the conversations between Burke in Washington and Cat Brown in the Sixth Fleet.[‡] "Whose side are we on?" You've heard that. "I'll let you know when I found out."[§]

Among other things, what the Sixth Fleet amphibious ships did was go into Alexandria and bring off—pick a number—800, 1,000 U.S. and friendly foreign nationals. The messages were absolutely lovely. He drove his chaplain nuts, but he got

---

[*] Fort Hood is in Texas; Fort Lewis is in Washington.
[†] On 6 November 1956 President Dwight D. Eisenhower was reelected, defeating his Democratic challenger, Adlai E. Stevenson.
[‡] Vice Admiral Charles R. Brown, USN, commanded the Sixth Fleet from August 1956 to 30 September 1958.
[§] For the exchange between Burke and Brown, see E.B. Potter, Admiral Arleigh Burke (New York: Random House, 1990), pages 414-415.

the quotation. The report of the completion of that—I don't know what it was, a biblical quotation, Exodus or something. When you looked it up, it said, "I have come to deliver them from the hand of the Egyptians." You've probably heard that before too. But what he did was plunk himself halfway between the airfields on Cyprus and the Suez Canal, and then he issued a notice to everybody, which was obviously to the British and the French: "A hundred miles around my ships, don't come in." So they had to dogleg the whole bloody time. That's a good illustration of flexibility.

There was another one two years later, a quite different time, in the Lebanese affair.[*] I forget the ambassador's name. He asked for the Marines.

Paul Stillwell: McClintock.

Admiral Wylie: McClintock. Then he was on the beach waving them to turn back. One of the first officers ashore explained to him, "At this moment, Mr. Eisenhower is making the announcement that we're here. We're not going back."

There were a couple of lesser incidents than that that have no lessons for them. One is that Admiral Holloway was then Commander in Chief Eastern Atlantic and Mediterranean.[†] He arrived on the scene early, probably in his AGC.[‡] I was in Washington at this time. After the Marines had gotten across the beach, Admiral Holloway wanted to take them up towards Beirut, which is up to the north of the landing site, which is right outboard at the airfield. I presume that's where the Marines were a couple of years ago, the same airfield.

But General Chehab was the head of the Army—he was, I guess, the Muslim part.[§] They always had a Christian President and a Muslim general, or vice versa, in the relatively orderly years before the present decade. Chamoun was the President. He had

---

[*] On 15 July 1958, at the request of Lebanese President Camille Chamoun, U.S. amphibious forces landed at Beirut to support Chamoun's government, which was threatened by both civil war and the prospect of foreign invasion. Two of the Sixth Fleet's three battalion landing teams went ashore within 24 hours. For details see the account of the U.S. ambassador to Lebanon, Robert McClintock, "The American Landing in Lebanon," U.S. Naval Institute Proceedings, October 1962, pages 64-79.
[†] Admiral James L. Holloway, Jr., USN, served as Commander in Chief U.S. Naval Forces Eastern Atlantic and Mediterranean (CinCNELM) and USComEastLant from February 1958 to March 1959.
[‡] AGC was the designation for an amphibious force flagship.
[§] General Fouad Chehab, who later replaced Camille Chamoun as President of Lebanon after elections in Parliament on 31 July 1958.

gone to the embassy the night before and asked for Marines. Admiral Holloway wanted the Marines up in Beirut, and there were General Chehab's Army forces across the road; they weren't going to let anybody by. So what nobody realized on the Lebanese side was that Admiral Holloway had been dealing with the Congress for 20 or 30 years, and he was as clever a double-dealer as any Lebanese that ever came down the pike. So he lined all his Marines up, had them lined up, walked over, invited General Chehab to review them.

They both got in a Jeep. Admiral Holloway was a fairly good-sized man—both sitting in the back of the Jeep. So with the guest of honor on his right, Admiral Holloway put his arm across General Chehab's shoulder, told the driver to go to Beirut, and held down General Chehab. And the troops saw the general there and made way, and the troops followed him right on out. He just held him down, and every time he'd squirm, he'd just press down harder, and Chehab couldn't be undignified about this. He couldn't put up a squabble, so the troops just opened up when they saw their boss, and they went on up to Beirut. Somebody was very clever.

I was not present. I was in Washington on this end of the dispatches, and I don't know where Admiral Holloway set up his headquarters ashore, but he had telephone taps on Chamoun and Chehab's headquarters, which made it very much less complicated than it would otherwise have been. How he got them, I don't know. But eventually that was resolved. It outgrew itself. People came down from Europe to get in the act. It got too big, more than was necessary, but it worked. Again, the flexibility. Now, what nobody knows is by in part good luck, and in part by delaying them a couple of weeks because it just looked wrong, we didn't have one embarked Marine battalion in the Mediterranean; we had two. The outgoing battalion had been held. That's happened before. It did not happen in '56. We had no warning. But things were brewing in Beirut at the time. I don't know who did it or brought it to Admiral Burke's attention, but the outgoing battalion had been held over. That happened several times later. It's real handy to have that second battalion afloat.

Paul Stillwell: There's one additional point that might be made, though, in speaking to future generations. Admiral Burke had more flexibility to maneuver forces than a CNO would now.[*]

Admiral Wylie: Yes and no. The technique would be a little different now. It would have to be done through the unified commanders rather than directly to the fleet. Don't forget, the only unified commanders that make any difference, there's only three. One is SAC out in Omaha, the other is CinCLant, and the other is CinCPac.[†] All these others are irrelevant. They come and go. So a telephone call to two unified commanders, and you could set in motion anything you want. They all know the CNO's their boss. They all know each other; they work together. It could be done. Although the technique would be different, the result could be total cooperation.

Paul Stillwell: I don't know, though, if you'd have a CNO who would go off like that on his own without bringing the rest of the JCS in on it.

Admiral Wylie: That's the crux of it. But the way the bloody thing is organized now, if my memory serves, the unified commanders work for the Secretary of Defense. Look that up sometime.

Paul Stillwell: I think it's supposed to go through or with the advice of the JCS.

Admiral Wylie: Yes. But check on it. It's screwed up like a Marine fire drill. It would be workable if the CNO wanted it to work that way; that's all I can say. He might not be a man with the verve and imagination of Burke, but if he wanted to work like that, he

---

[*] The Department of Defense Reorganization Act of 1958 contained a number of provisions, including removal of the service secretaries from the chain of command; removal of the service chiefs' command authority over their forces; establishment of the principle that the Joint Chiefs of Staff could act only under the authority of the Secretary of Defense; and transfer of control of the Joint Staff from the JCS as a whole to the Chairman.

[†] SAC stood for Strategic Air Command, which has since been replaced by the joint Strategic Command. In fact, the overall command structure has changed a good bit since this interview was conducted.

could, because the two critical unified commanders are in the two oceans, and the telephone you can't stop, covered or not, you know.[*]

Two other examples. I was in London at the time of the Greek coup, whatever that colonel's name was.[†]

Paul Stillwell: The one in '67.

Admiral Wylie: Yes, I think so. Mid-'60s. I guess I have to go back a little bit. The normal organization in, let us say, a big staff, has intelligence in one pocket and operations in another, and plans rarely sees them both. In London, thanks to dear Jimmy Thach, I put the intelligence watch officer in the same room with the operations watch officer, simply because I thought it was better.[‡] A lot of people do, a lot of people don't, particularly the intelligence people, who don't like information going adrift. But we had a bunch of young lieutenants, half a dozen of them, nice kids, smart, and the problem was, what instructions do they have? You said yesterday you didn't know an A-scope, you know, where the little bug runs along the line.[§] Well, this was the illustration I used. I think Hatch was the intelligence officer, a good captain.[**] I said, "Look, kids, just see everything, and if it's what you expected to see on all this traffic, that's all right. What you're really looking for is a spike on that radarscope, something that sticks up above, that catches your eye, that looks as though it's out of the pattern, that looks as though you didn't expect it, or something aberrant.

Well, I guess it was Sunday night. I lived four or five blocks from headquarters in London, and a young man called up about 8:00 o'clock. He said, "Sir, I got a spike."

I said, "Okay, I'll be down. Call Captain Hatch," and he already had, quite properly, his boss.

---

[*] The former unified Atlantic Command has since been replaced by an organization known as Joint Forces Command, another part of the move toward greater jointness that has taken place since this interview.
[†] A junta of Greek military officers, led by Colonel George Papadopoulos, seized control of the government on 21 April 1967. The Papadopoulos regime was ousted on 25 November 1973.
[‡] Admiral John S. Thach, USN, served as Commander in Chief U.S. Naval Forces Europe and Commander in Chief U.S. Naval Forces Eastern Atlantic from March 1965 to May 1967. Thach's oral history is in the Naval Institute collection.
[§] The A-scope was the linear type of radarscope presentation used early in World War II, before the circular PPI presentation came into use. Targets showed up as spikes along a horizontal line.
[**] Captain William M. Hatch, USN.

We went down there, and this was an NSA intercept of a telephone conversation between Cyprus and Athens.* There was no indication as to who was on each end of the telephone, but the substance of it was, "Everything is set for Friday." I don't know the words, but that was it. And this kid, bless his heart, that was the spike. What was set for Friday? He didn't know, so he phoned. He did exactly what he should have done. So we went over everything again, and there had been other cues of this coup coming in Greece, several of them, but none as definitive. So we talked it over that night and the next morning, everybody in the act, and we decided it was a coup—probably, not for certain, but probably.

Bill Martin was then Sixth Fleet Commander, and we had a back channel communication, which I assume you identify.† It's a radio communication not for the record. Actually, it's one of the intelligence circuits, but you don't put things on the record. We had a long discussion with Bill Martin, and the upshot of was, he would sort of move toward Greece, but he wouldn't pull any ships out of port early, and he wouldn't make any announcements. So his ships which were not in port also gravitated towards the southwest corner of the Aegean there. By Monday evening we'd become pretty sure what this was. You put a lot of mosaic tiles together, and you form, really, a judgment that would be hard to defend in court, but it works up.

So Monday and Tuesday the Sixth Fleet sort of ambled over toward the southwest corner of the Aegean, down below whatever it was, the Cyclades, those lower left-hand corner islands. On Wednesday we decided we'd better tell some other people, so we sent a message to, obviously, OpNav, not the Defense Intelligence Agency, not the Joint Staff, because we were not in the joint chain of command then. They are now—USCinCEur, Army Europe, Air Force. We were Navy, and that message went out Wednesday morning. And somebody, of course—as we knew they would—sent it on to the Defense Intelligence Agency. They spent all day Wednesday and all day Thursday arguing with each other on the air, messages to everybody, and finally deciding Thursday afternoon that this really didn't have enough validity.

---

* NSA—National Security Agency.
† Vice Admiral William I. Martin, USN, commanded the Sixth Fleet from April 1967 to 14 August 1968. His oral history is in the Naval Institute collection.

Well, of course, the coup came Friday morning. In the meantime, we had been gathering the same kind of information that we had gathered at Santo Domingo—who and where were the U.S. citizens and the friendly foreign nationals? On that occasion, it became apparent very early in our digging about that we might have to pull the King out, because he was on our side.* As it turned out, we didn't, but among the other items that we turned up, some not surprisingly, was that he was not in Athens. He was up north of Athens at the Tatoy Palace, 20-30 miles, and, secondly, that the Queen was about six or seven months pregnant, ergo, a problem. Now, as soon as Bill Martin heard that, he snaffled an obstetrician out of the Navy medical unit at Naples, flew him out to the carrier. I suspect that poor man doesn't know to this day why he was sent out to the carrier, but there he was.

We also found out that the Army had—you're not going to believe this—two field nuclear weapons caches in central Greece and one in northern Greece, not on the coast. God knows why. I don't remember that. So what did we do? We put some Marines in some LSDs and some fast vehicles.† They ambled up into the Aegean, close to a place where they could get ashore, but they just stayed. Nobody knew who was in them, what they were doing. It was easy. Of course, Friday, when the whole thing blew, why, the ambassador started screaming to his naval attaché, "Where's the fleet?"

And the only answer that we were permitted to send back was, "What is it that you want done? Why do you want the fleet? What for? What jobs are there?" And there were none. As it turned out, it was not necessary to extract the King. It was not necessary to go after the two Army ammunition dumps up in northern Greece. It wasn't necessary, really, to do anything. But the point of the tale is, no matter what had happened, we had a carrier within helicopter range of the Tatoy Palace. We had a list on the carrier of the palace hangers-on and who was to be extracted and who was not. The whole apparatus, it was marvelous. As it turned out, nobody had to do anything, but the point of the recital is, we could have. Nobody, I suppose, in Greece to this day knows we were ready to work.

---

* King Constantine II became the Greek monarch in 1964. After the coup of 21 April 1967 he retained his title but was powerless. In December of that year he tried to overthrow the military junta but failed, at which point he and his family fled the country and went to Italy.
† LSD—dock landing ship—a type of amphibious warfare ship with the capability of flooding down the stern section to launch or recover landing craft.

Paul Stillwell: There's another point worth mentioning—that you were able to fold the tent and move away quietly without having upset anybody.

Admiral Wylie: That's right. After the thing stabilized, and I think it didn't take too long for the U.S. Government to accept, if not recognize, Colonel Whatever-his-name-was, the new head colonel. We gradually backed out of sight, never were in sight, and it was a marvelous illustration of the flexibility of our service in readiness to serve whatever jobs may be assigned.

Paul Stillwell: There was another event that occurred almost at the same time that involved the Sixth Fleet, and that was the attack on the Liberty.* What do you recall about that episode?

Admiral Wylie: That had to do with the '67 war. Again, there were some preliminary cues on that. That was not a surprise. For instance, during the week preceding that war—how confidential is this? Is it public knowledge from this point on?

Paul Stillwell: Presumably that's the ground rule. You can put a restriction on the release, but it should not be classified.

Admiral Wylie: Okay. Anyway, we were in London, Bill Martin in the Sixth Fleet, and all our friends were watching this. It was not a surprise. About four or five days, I guess, before the war started we saw some Egyptian gunboats moving the wrong way in the Suez Canal. It didn't make sense. We finally realized they were going around and trying to go up the Gulf of Aqaba. This was enough out of pattern to make pretty sure there was going to be a fight going on. At that time we had a Middle East Force consisting of an old seaplane tender and two destroyers. There had recently been organized a unified

---

* On 8 June 1967, during the Six-Day War between Israel and Egypt, Israeli aircraft and torpedo boats made a number of attacks on the U.S. communications intelligence ship Liberty (AGTR-5). Of the ship's crew of 297, 34 were killed and 171 wounded. Israel claimed that the attack on the Liberty was a case of mistaken identity. Many in the ship's crew were skeptical of the claim.

command based in Tampa, of all places. It was headed by an Army officer who was an ass, and whose main interest was gathering power. For reasons I don't recall, if I ever knew, the Middle East Force was under his command. God knows why, but it was.

But it was a naval officer running it.[*] I did not know the man, a flag officer I'd never met, but it looked to us in London—and Bill Martin agreed with us; it was his fleet that was involved—as if this guy might need more than his two destroyers. Fortunately, we had a relief that came from the Sixth Fleet. So we sent the two southbound ones through, and then, again on the back channel—so that Tampa wouldn't get involved, no communication of record—we suggested to the guy in the Middle East Force that he not let his homeward-bound destroyers get north of Jidda, which is less than halfway up the Red Sea. So our two got south. As a result, when the thing finally blew and the canal was closed, he had four destroyers, and only then did anybody tell Tampa.[†] You know, he couldn't do anything about it then. They had to come home around Africa, by the way.

Paul Stillwell: In addition, the carrier Intrepid was on her way to Vietnam.

Admiral Wylie: She went through, yes. The destroyers, I think, went through the day after the Intrepid did. That was a conscious decision to send the Intrepid through.

I don't know how to say this, because nobody knows it yet. Liberty was not alone. Her companion was pulled out.

Paul Stillwell: Why?

Admiral Wylie: Because it looked wrong. Admiral Thach had been relieved by that time. His successor was a friend of mine, was very ambitious, and anxious not to ruffle any feathers, my boss at that time.

---

[*] Rear Admiral Walter L. Small, Jr., USN, served as Commander Middle East Force from 1 May 1967 to 11 June 1968.
[†] As a result of the Six-Day Arab-Israeli War in June 1967, the Suez Canal was blocked by sunken ships. It reopened in June 1975. See J. Huntly Boyd, "Nimrod Spar: Clearing the Suez Canal," U.S. Naval Institute Proceedings, February 1976, pages 18-26.

Paul Stillwell: Admiral McCain.*

Admiral Wylie: Yes. He had been in Germany when I pulled the other ship out. I don't know even whether we told him it was there, and we pulled it out, because it was a covert operation. But Liberty was under, as you know, an appalling, imprecise set of orders, at the end of an absolutely unmanageable chaos of communication. I know that our staff begged McCain to pull Liberty. He claimed he didn't have the authority. Enough said. He should have. And she was plugged.

Paul Stillwell: You say there was another ship with her. Do you mean another intelligence ship or a combatant, or both?

Admiral Wylie: Both. Yes, it was a submarine, which are very useful in those situations, especially if they're rigged as this one was. But we just pulled it the hell out of there, and this didn't even turn up in Ike Kidd's—you know, he held an inquiry afterwards, an investigation.† He could tell you more about this than any man I know. I hope you've seen him.

Paul Stillwell: He is, for whatever reason, leery of the oral history process.‡

Admiral Wylie: I'm sorry. He did a very good job in that in a variety of ways.

Anyway, I've said two things here. I've talked about the employability of naval forces. I've also talked about some pretty free-wheeling employment of intelligence, working on hints and cues, subjective judgments, and the "Well, let's do it" attitude. This, I think, is very important. I hope the kids have it in the years to come, because we're the only people who can do that without notoriety. I've given you a half a dozen examples of it. It's very important.

---

* Admiral John S. McCain, Jr., USN, served as Commander in Chief U.S. Naval Forces Europe and Commander in Chief U.S. Naval Forces Eastern Atlantic from May 1967 to July 1968.
† Rear Admiral Isaac C. Kidd, Jr., USN.
‡ Kidd eventually became a four-star admiral and retired in 1978. Although he was invited to do so several times, he never agreed to do an oral history. He died in 1999.

Paul Stillwell: One thing I've heard about the Liberty situation is that the Israelis heard that the Sixth Fleet's aircraft were being scrambled from the carriers and that, perhaps, is what got them to back off and not finish the job.

Admiral Wylie: I don't know. I don't know. Of course, too, somebody may have recognized the ship. She was wearing colors.

Paul Stillwell: The contention of many is that they probably recognized those colors well in advance.

Admiral Wylie: What's the oasis on the north coast of the Sinai? It begins with A—the key point on the north coast of the Sinai Peninsula; it begins with A. It's featured in just about every single contest across the Sinai in biblical times. Arish in English. God knows what it is in Arabic.

Paul Stillwell: I have heard of that.

Admiral Wylie: It's about halfway across, a little more than halfway east from the Suez to where the Levant coast turns north. The Bible people fought over el-Arish, Napoleon used it, it was used during World War I. Every time it's the key point in the Arab-Israeli squabbles. It has a long history, is crucial. I don't know why I brought it up, except that's where the Liberty was. She was off el-Arish, and that's where the Israeli headquarters was.

Paul Stillwell: While we're on the topic of your time in that billet, I'd be interested in your recollections of both Admiral Thach and Admiral McCain.

Admiral Wylie: I'll speak about Thach. I loved him dearly. He was a good, commonsense, gentle, sensible man. He spent most of his time down in the country playing golf. He had retired without telling the Bureau of Personnel, perfectly normal. He was satisfied with his staff, so why the hell should he bother with it? Mrs. Thach was not well at that time. She preferred it down in the country. You are aware that there is a country house that went with the job?

Paul Stillwell: No, I wasn't.

Admiral Wylie: Yes. That dates from World War II also, not far from—where's the race course, Ascot, out west of London in the country, right next to the golf course that every three or four years has one of the British open tournaments—lovely. The State Department's been trying to get it for years. They may have by now. They want it for the ambassador. But, anyway, the commander in chief at that time had a flat above the headquarters there, at the corner there of Grosvenor Square at North Audley Street, and the country house. I just loved Jimmy Thach. He just never crossed up his staff once he learned who they were and what their capabilities were. It was just the most delightful thing in the world to serve with him.

Paul Stillwell: It gave you a chance to be in charge, didn't it?

Admiral Wylie: Sure—for practical purposes, me and my friend Bill Martin on the other end of the line in the Mediterranean. We had worked together, we understood each other, we trusted each other, and we just got along fine.

Paul Stillwell: Wasn't Admiral Thach a little out of his element in that? He was an airplane and tactics man.

Admiral Wylie: There's another facet to that job. I think the last commander in chief, Navy, in London who really understood it was Page Smith.[*] A principal task is the support of the RN, who had come on parlous times at the end of World War II. I had acquired that feeling from Admiral Smith as a friend. Jimmy Thach didn't care much for

---

[*] Admiral Harold P. Smith, USN, served as Commander in Chief U.S. Naval Forces Eastern Atlantic and Mediterranean (CinCNELM), U.S. Commander Eastern Atlantic, and Commander in Chief U.S. Naval Forces Europe (CinCUSNavEur) from February 1960 to April 1963.

entertainment and this sort of thing, and the result was gorgeous for Mrs. Wylie and me. We did a great portion of the entertaining.

At that time the First Sea Lord was a man named Varyl Begg.[*] He was at dinner at our house one night, and the RN—this was under the period of Denis Healey as the Minister of Defence, who was a patsy for McNamara and a really dreadful man, without much common sense and glib as hell, but, anyway, the RN was in deep trouble.[†] During dinner I said, "Gee, it's a long time since I've seen anything, speeches in the House of Commons to give the Navy a hand." Admiral Begg agreed. I said, "Good heavens, can't you induce some? It would help." There was budget trouble as usual, which is perfectly normal for any service.

He sort of bridled, the implication being that one doesn't, you know. The old school.

I said, "Admiral, would you like a couple of good speeches?"

"Oh, yes," he said, "I wish some of our friends would speak out."

So I said, "I'll get you some." Sometimes you're brash. So for about two or three evenings, about 6:00 o'clock, I'd go down to the RNVR Club, just off South Audley Street, past that China store, Booth's.[‡] It's not far from South Audley Street, about four or five blocks. They were very kind, and we, the USN, at least I was, a nice car down at the ship, the RNVR Club, this is the wavy Navy. I went down there and sat with a beer at the bar for a couple of nights, and, sure enough, I encountered a couple of MPs.[§] I told them what the problem was, and we got two cracking good, tub-thumping speeches in the Commons. Well, the result of it was that Begg sent his PR guy over for a course at our headquarters.

Another illustration of how to help the RN. Seven sisters. There was an oiler grounded in the Scilly Isles.[**] You may recall that. I forget its name. Anyway, there

---

[*] Admiral Sir Varyl C. Begg, RN, served as Great Britain's First Sea Lord and Chief of Naval Staff from 1966 to 1968.
[†] Denis Healey served as Great Britain's Minister of Defence from 1964 to 1970. Robert S. McNamara was U.S. Secretary of Defense from 21 January 1961 to 29 February 1968.
[‡] RNVR—Royal Navy Voluntary Reserve.
[§] MPs—members of Parliament.
[**] On 19 March 1967 the Liberian-flag, British-chartered, Italian-manned tanker Torrey Canyon grounded on the Seven Stones Reef between Lands End, England, and the Scilly Isles. She was sailing for Milford Haven with 120,000 gallons of Kuwaiti oil. The resulting spill created a 700-square-mile oil slick that damaged beaches in England, France, and Belgium.

was a colossal oil spill, the whole south coast of England. Quite to my surprise, Great Britain panicked. They didn't know what to do. They'd never thought of pollution control. So at the staff meeting one morning we sort of said, "What in the heck can we do to help the RN look good in this situation?"

We answered, somewhat surprising, that we had on that staff the best aerographer-meteorologist in the world—retired flag officer now, Bill Kotsch—and he was not only an aerographer, but he was a whiz on oceanography.[*] So twice a day he would prepare estimates of oil movement east along the south coast from Cornwall toward the channel, take it over to the RN. The RN would then put it into the British system, and it would go out as an RN contribution. It helped a great deal to raise the stature of the RN in that heavily Labour Government apparatus. At one point Bill Kotsch came in and said, "This thing is going to get over on the French coast on, let us say, Tuesday next," or whatever. So we wrote a dispatch to tell the U.S. naval attaché in Paris, so he could tell the French. The French turned up their bloody noses, paid no attention to it whatever, and panicked when the oil got there on schedule. I don't give a damn about the French; our job was to help the RN and help the English. But things like that can be very useful.

I had the great good fortune of being there while that marvelous man, the ambassador, one of the finest men I've ever met and surely the smartest—he was ambassador to Paris, Bonn, London, Peking, the Vatican.[†] Anyway, it'll come to me. I'm 74 years old, and I can't play these tapes as fast as I should. He lived outside of Baltimore. One of only two men I've ever known who could have comfortably been a colleague of the founding fathers. I'll get his name later. Anyway, I used to go over to his weekly conference, and the result was we were able to work very closely with him.

One interesting thing, which has nothing to do with being in the Navy. As I mentioned, we entertained more, I think, than most juniors would have in that situation, and also went out probably more than most juniors. The first time it happened, I thought

---

[*] Captain William J. Kotsch, USN. He has written books titled Weather for the Mariner (Annapolis: U.S. Naval Institute, 1970) and Heavy Weather Guide (Annapolis: U.S. Naval Institute, 1965).
[†] David K. E. Bruce served as U.S. Ambassador to the Court of St. James's from 22 February 1961 to 20 March 1969.

the guy was drunk—British businessman. The question was something like, "Do you think if we became a state we could retain the monarchy?"

The next time, the question turned up from another man: "Do you think we could become four states?" You get the flavor of what I'm saying. After about three or four of these, over a period of, say, three or four months—not long after I got there, as a matter of fact—I went over to see the ambassador, and he said, "Yes, they don't ask me, but they ask my minister."

I said, "What in the hell do you tell them, Mr. Ambassador?"

He said, "There's nothing you can tell them. They're just tired after two World Wars, the dreadful drumming they've taken, they just want to shed responsibility." Startling, isn't it? I got plenty more after that, another half a dozen. Similar questions—how could they turn the whole apparatus over to the United States? This is mid-'60s. I'd think they'd do it now. Maybe they will. But absolutely fascinating and heartbreaking. They wouldn't ask Jim; he was the head man. They wouldn't ask the ambassador; he was the head man. But they'd ask number two, the minister and me. And they weren't all drunk either, not by a long shot.

Paul Stillwell: Did Thach make a nominal number of appearances at obligatory functions?

Admiral Wylie: Yes, yes. He didn't neglect anything. He and Mrs. Thach just didn't feel like going more than they thought was necessary. Okay, that left a lot of fun for us.

Paul Stillwell: You said he was followed by an ambitious flag officer. What difference did that make in operating style?

Admiral Wylie: Everything.

Paul Stillwell: What did it do to your role?

Admiral Wylie: I became ancillary. I didn't stay long. In the normal course, it would have come. It came a little sooner than it might have. He had to have an aviator as number two, because he was not, as Thach was. I'm sorry that's not classified.

Paul Stillwell: What else do you have on your list?

Admiral Wylie: Let me see. This is between chores in the morning. The '56 and '58 wars. It's perfectly normal in OpNav now; they have an operations center. In 1956 there was none. First I'd better explain how Admiral Burke worked. Some of his flag officers were tuned in to him. More of them thought he was erratic. What it really was, they were conservative where he was not. He had trouble with some of his flag officers. He had trouble finding out what the kids thought in OpNav, and he put great store by young people, lieutenant commanders. He put a lieutenant commander in almost every section of OpNav, certainly in plans and operations, just simply because he wanted to bring them right up.

I was a four-striper at the time, so it was way below. But he had half a dozen four-stripers whom he used both for test firing and as whipping boys. Martin was one; he was his aide.[*] George Miller was one.[†] McCain was one.[‡] Colonel Lou Frank was one, a Marine.[§] There were a couple of others. When he was totally frustrated, he'd get one or more of these four-stripers and send them off to do a job which was practically impossible, because the flag officers in the various divisions weren't cut in on this. As often as not, when he'd become totally frustrated with something, he'd fire a four-striper: "Get out of my office. Don't come back." And sometimes you weren't summoned back for as long as a week. You see what I'm telling you.

Paul Stillwell: Forever lasted a week.

---

[*] Captain William I. Martin, USN, served as executive assistant and senior aide to the Chief of Naval Operations from January 1956 to July 1957.
[†] Captain George H. Miller, USN. The oral history of Miller, who retired as a rear admiral, is in the Naval Institute collection.
[‡] Captain John S. McCain, Jr., USN. See the Naval Institute oral history of Vice Admiral Thomas R. Weschler, USN (Ret.), for a marvelous anecdote involving Burke and McCain.
[§] Colonel Louis L. Frank, USMC.

Admiral Wylie: Okay. When the '56 thing blew, he had his usual conference, which—these were all flag officers, practically, and right after that, he summoned four or five four-stripers into his office, not in the conference room, and talked over this thing, as presumably he'd just done with others. And then his question was, "What do we do?"

Well, I said, "Admiral, you need a CIC."

And he said, "All right, go start it." Well, it took me a little while to get a specific instruction. The most important feature was I could have any officer in OpNav that I wanted, by his direction. Well, what that meant, I could raid Admiral This and Admiral That and take his best four-striper. Well, we got it set up by that afternoon, and it lasted and served, I think, fairly well, mostly as a briefing room for people who needed segments of information, as well as all of it. When you go around stealing a flag officer's best four-striper, you don't endear yourself.

About a month after the '56 thing had settled down, there was enough grumbling that it was abolished, and, of course, we had to start all over again in 1958. That time it stuck. Presumably, by now it's a hallowed organization, and it's shaken down, and it's not fly by night. But we were talking about the correlation of information yesterday with respect to the CIC handbook for destroyers. We had to do exactly the same thing, but not in that context, in 1956 for the Suez war and again in 1958 in OpNav. It stuck the second time.

Paul Stillwell: Who were some of these people that you robbed to fulfill that function?

Admiral Wylie: I haven't the faintest idea. I don't remember. They were all pleased to sort of get in the act, and I had no trouble with three- and four-stripers. It was only the flag officers who were grumpy. But I'll say one thing—Admiral Burke always backed up his people. If they gave us too hard a time, he'd calm them down. But, anyway, that was the genesis of—I don't know what they call it now. It must be an OpNav or a CNO operations center now; I don't know what it is. I haven't the faintest idea.

Paul Stillwell: That's probably the exact title.

Admiral Wylie: Whatever. But, anyway, it started in '56, it fell apart, and it started again in '58 and stuck, and that's all I know. I told you Burke closed in on the Middle East, all around the world.

After the 1956 war, the other services were sore. They felt frustrated, because only Burke could move forces. Mistakenly, they thought it was because the law gave him command. It did. He commanded the naval forces of the United States. The Chief of Staff of the Army—under law, his only task was to preside over the Army staff. Believe it or not, it's still true today. The Chief of Staff of the Air Force presided over the air staff; they didn't have command. They mistakenly thought that because Burke had command under law, that was why he did all these things. The real reason, of course, is that a Navy is employable, a sea-based force is, a land-based force is not. So the result was that the 1958 reorganization plan took that away from the Navy. That was because of what happened in '56. Has anybody told you of that Burke session with his colleagues about a month after the '56 affair?

Paul Stillwell: No.

Admiral Wylie: Well, the deputies were there. That's how it leaked out. They all ganged up on him for not keeping them fully informed and getting their advice on what he was doing, and finally he said, "Do you know the story of the Shan?"

Have I gotten anything familiar yet?

Paul Stillwell: No.

Admiral Wylie: And he said, "Well, the Shan is the crown prince, the son of the Shah, and the Shan was subject to epileptic fits. So the Shah decided he'd better put a watch on this young man, somebody to take care of him and get him out of sight when he's had epilepsy. So he had a bevy of young women. The young Shan was making a speech one day, and the epilepsy caught him. He fell down, writhing on the platform. Everybody could see him. The Shah was furious, and he summoned this bevy of women and said, "Goddamn it, where were you when the fit hit the Shan?"

Well, his colleagues wouldn't talk to him for a month. That may have had something to do with the '58 legislation also. (I hope your typist is tolerant.)

Paul Stillwell: You sucked me in.

Admiral Wylie: Well, he sucked the chiefs in, you bet. That was his story.

I think I've got everything there. One more thing. I'd like to go back to yesterday. I told you we got this destroyer handbook, <u>CIC Handbook for Destroyers</u>. It's really hard to believe today that as far as I can find out, that's the first document that ever tried to gather all sources of information together to serve the captain of a ship. As I said, we printed 500 and went to 15,000 in six weeks. But its principle—forward half was current events, the back half was history, or vice versa. One half was air, the other half was surface, and we had submarine stuff in between them. I have no idea what a CIC looks like today, but I bet even if it's distorted for convenience in putting in a ship, you'll find that correlation.

Paul Stillwell: It certainly does look different, from what I hear.

Admiral Wylie: It's probably chock-a-block with computers. But what are computers? Are they historical data that you call up—history being ten minutes ago—if you want? Or are they current events? I bet, without having seen one in 20 years, you'll find that same conceptual arrangement.

Now, another thing I haven't talked about, and, again, I'm putting this into your system, because some youngster some time may want to know about it. When I mentioned that I couldn't get a carrier exec's job at the end of the war, and they wouldn't give me an aviator for my destroyer exec, to go back to sea—I'd been at sea all during the war, except for the last two months in that special defense section—I found a job in ONR, and as it turned out, it was probably the first of the human engineering research activities.[*] I think the current word, and it's used in auto advertising, is ergonomic. Work spaces correlation. What can a man see and remember? What can he read? What

---

[*] ONR—Office of Naval Research.

can you learn by touch? For instance, at the end of that project, there was a primitive sort of handbook for design engineers—knobs, different shapes, what can you tell tactilely, say in an airplane cockpit? How many items can you remember if you see pips on a scope? Seven, by the way. Beyond that, you lose count. You can identify seven with a glance. Color discrimination, this sort of thing that's good for design engineers.

When I figured that the demobilization was over, I guess 1946, '7, and '8, I got my job abolished. I had originally six, later down to two or three universities on the string. Johns Hopkins was the principal contractor. And it was fun, but I decided to come back into the Navy when the demobilization was over, and since I was living here in Newport—the laboratory was over on the tip of Beaver Tail at Jamestown. Why? Because it was available, I guess.

I got orders to the war college as a student. Towards the end of that one-year course, there were half a dozen of us up on that third floor of one of the old buildings where the have a checkerboard floor where there used to be war games. We were uncomfortable, because the service differences were really beginning to blow up. We had just had the Unification Act.[*] Really, nobody could decently answer the question, "Why do we have a Navy?" You ought to think about that before you agree with me.

Paul Stillwell: The Air Force said we didn't need one.

Admiral Wylie: That's right. All we could do was say, Goddamn it, we can do it," or, "Goddamn it, we can do it better." You know, a positive statement, which is predecessor to the flat denial. We sort of informally agreed that the first one of us that came back ought to start an effort to find out why we have a Navy. George Miller was one; Bill Moffett was one. I forget who the others were. It doesn't make any difference. He was a nice man, by the way, and I haven't seen him since—Moffett, I mean.[†] He was in '30.

---

[*] The National Security Act of 1947 became effective on 18 September of that year. It provided for the unification of the services under the aegis of a single National Military Establishment, which later became the Department of Defense. Previously the Secretaries of War and Navy had been Cabinet officials. Now there were three different departments at sub-Cabinet level: Army, Navy, and Air Force. As part of the act the former U.S. Army Air Forces became a separate service, the U.S. Air Force.

[†] Captain William A. Moffett, Jr., USN.

His daddy was a pioneer aviator.* I knew nothing of carriers, because Moffett was an aviator, the younger Moffett, the guy in '30.

But, anyway, I went off to San Diego and got orders back to the war college staff a year later and was halfway across the country when the Korean thing broke.† I spent the whole Korean War, three years, at the war college. But, anyway, I got back there, and not long after I got back, I encountered a then reserve Lieutenant Commander, Gene Burdick, whom you may or may not identify.

Paul Stillwell: He was coauthor of The Ugly American.‡

Admiral Wylie: That's right. Most people connect him with that. He was one of the very few Rhodes scholars ever to get his doctorate in political philosophy, which is at the apex of the academic triangle. A very bright man.

About that time I went to Admiral Conolly, and I had sketched out—you know, you do things on paper, three or four officers whom he would turn loose for a couple of years to figure out why we had a Navy.§ Admiral Conolly latched onto that notion. I guess every president likes a new idea. Somewhat unfortunately, he expanded it, and it was cursed with the title of "the course of advanced study in strategy and sea power." Well, this was top-heavy. It wasn't that. But, anyway, what he did was give us the rest of that year, which was the first of the three years I was back there. He told me I could have Burdick, who was the public affairs officer—you know, waste. So Burdick and I traveled up and down the East Coast, and we talked to a lot of people in universities. How do we figure out why we have a Navy? Two of them gave us the same answer in totally different form, and in each of them it was so damn abstruse and complicated that it took us until the next day to sort out our notes and figure what these two men had told us.

---

* Rear Admiral William A. Moffett, USN, served as Chief of the Bureau of Aeronautics from 26 July 1921 until his death on 4 April 1933.
† The Korean War began on 25 June 1950, when six North Korean infantry division and three border constabulary brigades invaded the South Korea. The troops were supported by approximately 100 Russian-made T-34 tanks. In New York that same day the United Nations Security Council adopted a resolution condemning the invasion.
‡ William J. Lederer and Eugene L. Burdick, The Ugly American (New York: Norton, 1958). It is a powerful novel that deals with the impression that Americans make in countries overseas.
§ Vice Admiral Richard L. Conolly, USN, served as president of the Naval War College from 1 December 1950 to 2 November 1953.

One was a man named Laswell at the Yale Law School. He'd been a sociologist, a political scientist, an economist, and ended up at the Yale Law School. And he was the most abstruse man I've ever encountered. The other man, who told us exactly the same thing in a totally different fashion was John von Neuman, the mathematician at the Institute for Advanced Study at Princeton. What they said was, "If you're going to figure out why you have a Navy, you have to have a theory, and if you have a theory, you have to have a vocabulary with which to talk about it, and you don't have either. Get to work." Totally impossible.

We laid out a course. Admiral Conolly got ordered, I think, 10 or 11 officers, including one flag officer, Rear Admiral Ralph Earle, Jr. And the way we decided to do it, you start with a premise. Naval officers, by and large, are very good, indeed, at managing concrete facts and data and things. They are totally, or nearly so, untrained in the manipulation of ideas.

So we had a series of five people from various universities, from Harvard to Johns Hopkins: an historian who was a beauty, political scientist who was useful, an economist from Harvard who had no idea what we were after, a geographer, and a sociologist, I think. The problem we sent them, "You have a week. Tell us how your discipline manages ideas." Well, the geographer tried to make instant geographers out of us, and so on. The economist from Harvard, a man with a harelip—I forget his name; he's quite famous now—tried to make instant economists out of us. But the historian and the political scientist sensed what we were after and were fairly useful. The historian, by the way, was Tom Mendenhall, who was then at Yale and later became president of a girls' university.[*]

And at the same time, each of the, I think, ten of us, had once a week to select a subject, prepare an argument, and defend it. When we started out, everybody was a little reluctant to be utterly nasty to his colleagues. It took us a couple of months to get over that—you know, in a seminar session, take a position and defend it, and everybody else try to tear it down. Well, when we got used to that, it became very useful, once we got over our courtesy, intellectually speaking.

---

[*] Dr. Thomas C. Mendenhall II was for many years a professor of history at Yale University; in 1959 he became president of Smith College in Northampton, Massachusetts.

The result of it was probably at the end of the year, we had a better notion of how to identify and manipulate an idea. An illustration: the war college then had many more lecturers than they have now, and early on, General LeMay came up.* He was then quite well known. What we got was, in effect, the SAC pitch. This is the early '50s—'51, yes. That was the time of the B-36 versus the carrier argument.† Of course, he infuriated everybody, and it was a shouting match in the question period, totally unproductive. We went to all the lectures, this small group of mine. At the end of the year, General White came up.‡ He was then the Vice Chief of the Air Force and was quite generally recognized as the smartest of the general officers there and vastly more smooth than General LeMay. He gave what was, in effect, the SAC pitch. One of our guys stood up and said, "General White, you have said this, and you have said that, and from that you have said this. And under it all is this assumption." I don't remember that it was, but it absolutely devastated General White's idea. It just cut the underpinnings out of him. General White stared at him a minute and walked offstage. He never came back. So what I'm doing is illustrating how to handle ideas.

Anyway, for the second year of that course we took a subject; we continued with the seminars and the ideas. One guy took "Shoal and Inland Waters," another guy took "A Strategy for a Lesser Navy." The Marine obviously took "Why a Marine Corps?" or whatever was the terminology, and he produced about two inches by the year's end. I'm digressing now. For at least ten years after that, I could see direct quotations out of that in Marine generals' speeches. It served a useful purpose. We all took different but related subjects. Along about January, middle of the year, we were faced with the question, "What the hell are we going to do with this stuff when we get it?" And, of course, one obvious thing was, "Write an article for the Proceedings." Well, at that time, the Proceedings had less vitality than it has now, and it was paid less attention than now.

---

* General Curtis E. LeMay, USAF, served as Commander in Chief of the Strategic Air Command from 19 October 1948 to 30 June 1957. He was a lieutenant general until 29 October 1951. The original title was Commanding General, changed to Commander in June 1953 and changed to Commander in Chief in April 1955.
† In the late 1940s, the Navy and Air Force were competing for scarce defense dollars. Secretary of Defense Louis Johnson accelerated production of the Air Force's B-36 bomber and canceled the aircraft carrier United States (CVA-58) soon after the beginning of construction. The Navy fought back, as detailed in Jeffrey G. Barlow, Revolt of the Admirals (Washington, D.C.: Naval Historical Center, 1994).
‡ General Thomas D. White, USAF.

Finally, someone said, "Well, we'd better do other people's work for them. Let's write speeches and write op orders for people," which we volunteered to do. We wrote speeches for any senior in Washington who wanted a speech, and all their speechmakers knew it. We wrote the Atlantic and Pacific basic op orders. And the crux of it was—the purpose of the Navy is to extend power onto the land, not direct necessarily—indirect, subtle, not necessarily military, and so forth. Do I communicate?

I was not then and have not since then been able to find anything specifically to that effect in any writing prior to 1952. Corbett works all around it, but he never quite says it.[*] Corbett implied it, but he never said it. For instance, after I left there, I worked for Page Smith when he had an amphibious group.[†] Not long after I got there, I was, I think, his operations officer, middle-sized four-striper. He was tagged with giving the annual amphibious speech to the NATO Defense College.[‡] I said, "I'll write it for you." And the substance of it was, the purpose of the amphibious force is to extend control from the sea onto the land. It had a lot of other stuff, but that was the main point—why an amphibious force.

He came back, and I said, "How did it go?"

He said, "You won't believe it. You know, that speech was given in two languages. I spoke in English, and I gave a copy to the French translators, and they went along with me. The people listening in English understood what I was saying. The translator couldn't get it into French." The concept of control, the extension, and so forth. Well, anyway, we wrote the basic op order of the Atlantic Fleet, extend control onto the land, op orders for the PacFlt. We wrote dozens of speeches for the great and near-great. The theory of this is very simple. If a man hears what he says, he believes it. Ergo, we made our points. As far as I know, it's never been—yes, I had it in one essay in the Proceedings, but most people missed it.[§] But now it's common currency. People

---

[*] Julian S. Corbett (1854-1922) was an English lawyer and naval historian. After writing a few novels in the late 19th century he devoted himself to naval history and was a prolific author in that field. He wrote a three-volume set, Naval Operations, published in 1920, 1921, and 1923.
[†] Rear Admiral Harold Page Smith, USN, served as Commander Amphibious Group Two from November 1953 to February 1955.
[‡] NATO—North Atlantic Treaty Organization.
[§] Captain J. C. Wylie, Jr., USN, "On Maritime Strategy," U.S. Naval Institute Proceedings, May 1953, pages 467-477. The article was awarded honorable mention in the Naval Institute's General Prize Essay Contest that year.

think it was always that way, that's what a Navy's for, to extend power from the sea onto the land—economic, political, psychological, social, military, anything, and gradations of it influenced, probably, the more frequently encountered variant of control or degree of control. So we did get something useful out of that course, but nobody knows it.

I was detached at the end of my third year, one year of preparation, two years for the course, and by that time Admiral Conolly had retired and been killed in an aircraft accident.[*] I think Admiral Wallace Beakley is now dead.[†]

Paul Stillwell: Yes.

Admiral Wylie: He couldn't stand this eccentric class. It just drove him up the wall. Within a year, he had it turned into a problem-solving apparatus. The problems were in Washington, the solvers were in Newport. There was no connection, and it was a total failure. Another year, I guess, before it was abolished. I think probably the lesson to be learned is that an effort like that without a measurable product can't survive in a governmental arena, not necessarily Navy. Civil, if they had one. They'd need to measure the output in column inches or whatever, or reams, or something.

Paul Stillwell: It might have been useful had you produced something tangible like that.

Admiral Wylie: Well, I'm not sure. George Roe, the Marine, did, and the Marines used it.[‡] But within a period of, I would say, two years, this basic notion, which is now taken for granted by everybody, the extension or control of power, or whatever the terminology may be, from the sea onto the land, is the ultimate purpose. Everybody thinks it's always been there, which is really the best measure of its correctness. Do I communicate? Eventually it failed. I don't really think it could be repeated.

The only follow-on was, Bud Burdick went back to the graduate teaching at Berkeley, and he wrote me a couple of years later. He said, "When you get ready to

---

[*] Admiral Richard L. Conolly retired 1 November 1953 and died 1 March 1962. His oral history is in the Columbia University collection.
[†] Rear Admiral Wallace M. Beakley, USN, was Conolly's deputy at the Naval War College in the early 1950s. He retired as a vice admiral in January 1964 and died 16 January 1975.
[‡] Colonel Thomas George Roe, USMC.

retire, come on out, and we'll pick up that project at Berkeley. I have found an angel to underwrite it." I have no idea who it was. Not long after that, he had his first heart attack and misbehaved, and had a fatal heart attack at noon in the hot sun in San Diego, playing tennis.* He was dumb. He shouldn't have done it, but he died. I never found out who his angel was, and I never pursued it further. Yes, I have. The 1967 book and this manuscript are variations of pursuits of that period—not directly, but variations.†

During the Vietnam War we got a copy from somewhere. It may have been [unclear]. I don't know, whoever wrote "Shoal and Inland Waters." He slipped a copy of it to the peon in OpNav who had the Delta.‡ I don't know whether it ever did any good or not, but at least he had a basic document of a man who had thought long and hard about the many problems in this and had it hammered at by some good hammerers. I don't know whether it ever did any good or not. I know George Roe's did. I think, probably, that one did. I really don't know about the rest of them. At that time we lacked an organ. The Proceedings, as I say, was very pallid 35 years ago. The War College Review was certainly not exciting. It consisted of lectures by outsiders that somebody thought worth printing, nothing more. It's a live magazine now, but at that time it was simply a vehicle for printing unclassified lectures. There was no organ. I'm not at all sure whether it could be managed printing things like that—maybe today; we'll see.

Paul Stillwell: What's the filler, then, the time you spent with DesFlot 1? What were the events of that period?

Admiral Wylie: Nothing. Nothing notable. I guess that was Seventh Fleet, wasn't it?§ Of course, these aviators ran everything, because there was a carrier present. One day a friend of mine, the aviation flag officer, told me to handle the refueling. Well, by that time everybody had gotten timid, and refueling was a very laborious process. You sneaked up the side of the oiler and gradually crept into place, and you didn't go inside

---

* Burdick died in 1965.
† J. C. Wylie, Military Strategy: a General Theory of Power Control (New Brunswick, N.J., Rutgers University Press, 1967).
‡ This is a reference to the Mekong Delta in South Vietnam, where the United States fought a riverine war.
§ Admiral Wylie's answer here actually refers to his command of CruDesFlot 9 in the early 1960s.

100 or one million feet or something. So I just decided to do it like it'd been done 20 years earlier. I'd been there 20 years earlier.

Paul Stillwell: Even five.

Admiral Wylie: I don't know. But, anyway, I brought it in at 25 knots, morning light, turned them, went up behind them, and I didn't release anybody until the carrier had an overlap with the stern of the oiler. I could see it. He'd been asking and asking for release, and I wouldn't give it to him. Well, of course, he was frantic, and he backed full, which is exactly what he should have done. By the time he had slowed to 15 knots, he was in position. Totally irrelevant, totally unimportant, but that's about the only exciting thing.

Hong Kong. Hong Kong then, presumably now—then was 25 years ago—was what Shanghai had been in the '30s. It was the big, thriving, bustling center for international affairs. Everything moved to Hong Kong when Shanghai closed down. In the '30s Hong Kong was buttoned up tight at 9:00 o'clock, pure Victorian. Singapore was even worse; it buttoned up a sundown. I haven't seen Singapore since. Hong Kong is what China used to be. Manila then, and probably now, is like Los Angeles. It's a city without a focus, without a character; it's a great sprawling mass. San Francisco has a character, a focus. Chicago has a focus; New York has a focus. Los Angeles doesn't, and Manila doesn't. It's a great amorphous mass of people.

Fun. Absolutely irrelevant. In 1935, in January, I was in Manila when the first Pan Am clipper came across the Pacific, cut from five weeks to five days, because they only flew in daylight: Philippines, Guam, Midway, Pearl, West Coast.[*] Big flying boats. We all knew the clipper was coming; we were all eager to watch for it. But what a surprise when the entire city had a spontaneous outburst of parading, whooping, hollering, and everything else. The whole city went wild when that silly, clumsy, old flying boat taxied up to the float in Manila. That was the first transpacific schedule.

---

[*] Pan Am—Pan American World Airways, which had a long, close association with the U.S. Navy. Its clippers were flying boats that could travel across the Pacific far faster than any ship.

Paul Stillwell: I see they've just now put out a new airmail stamp to commemorate the 50th anniversary.

Admiral Wylie: It was, I think, January. It might have been February of 1935. I didn't know they had a commemoration. Of course, like everybody else, I sent letters home with the special stamps at that time. I'd love to have them now. I think it cost 75 cents to send a letter or a dollar and a half, some appalling sum. This was in the era of three-cent mail, two or three cents, penny postcards. I guess it's $1.50 to send a letter now.

Paul Stillwell: The Navy relied a great deal on clipper mail to get its business done.

Admiral Wylie: Sure. Sure. I'll give you one other illustration of another subject that we haven't touched, and that's the naval officer as diplomat. I mentioned yesterday that Admiral Upham got his back up and gave the back of his hand to the Royal Highness, Duke of Gloucester, who was an appalling snob, by the way.

A later cruise must have been November of 1935 or thereabouts.* Anyway, the winter cruise of the Asiatic Fleet flagship had been down south of the Philippines, the Netherlands East Indies, Singapore, the Malay Peninsula, and we had been to Bangkok. I don't remember the name of the port. Bangkok is not on the sea, you know. It's 20, 40, 50 miles up the river. It was then a railroad. But, anyway, we had been to Bangkok and were over in Pontianak in British North Borneo, when there came a message from the ambassador in Bangkok: could we please come back? The problem was that a palace coup was brewing, and the antagonists in this—I forget which was ins and which was outs—were the British-educated Siamese and the U.S.-educated Siamese. Yes, the admiral, the commander in chief, please come back so you can help.

Well, at that time radio communications were not easy. When we were lucky—for instance, down in the Netherlands East Indies—we could reach Panama, not always. You know, this is a long time ago. Anyway, the admiral sent off a message to his master

---

* The ship's history for the USS Augusta indicates that she visited Bangkok from 15 to 22 October 1935; Singapore from 24 to 30 October; Pontianak, North Borneo, from 31 October to 1 November and Jesselton, North Borneo, 3 to 5 November. Admiral Orin G. Murfin, USN, had taken over command of the Asiatic Fleet on 5 October, shortly before this cruise began.

in Washington that he was going back to Bangkok. He didn't say why. They wrote their own ticket in those days. When we got back to whatever—I can't remember the name of the port—for Djakarta it was Tanjong Priok—but for Bangkok, anyway, the mouth of the river.[*] The admiral went up to the city and obviously talked it over with his lordship, the ambassador. On the second day, one of the two contingents came down by train and had lunch aboard ship with the admiral, and then went back. On the third day, the other contingent came down and had lunch. On the fourth day, the admiral went back to Bangkok. On the fifth day, both contingents came down and had lunch together in the cabin and made their peace.

Paul Stillwell: And on the sixth day the admiral rested.

Admiral Wylie: Not quite. On the sixth day, there was a celebration banquet in Bangkok, celebrating the reuniting or whatever, and every officer not on watch was ordered to go. We all went, and we were given suitable presents, a cigarette case or something in that Siamese mialloware [phonetic]. Then, on the seventh day, we left. But what I'm telling you is—and I'll give another illustration in a moment—a naval officer at sea, in his ship, is the United States, not accredited to any country.

Now, one of Page Smith's tasks when he first took his CinCNELM job, which later became CinCUSNavEur, was to visit his parish, and his parish included both India and Pakistan.[†] He stayed, I think, a little longer than he should have, shuffling back and forth between the two countries, because he was the only U.S. official, short of the Secretary of State, who had legitimate tickets to visit both countries officially. Do I make the point enough for your records?

Paul Stillwell: Yes, indeed.

---

[*] Djakarta is a city in Indonesia; it was formerly known as Batavia when the island was known as Java, part of the Dutch East Indies.

[†] In September 1958, Commander in Chief U.S. Naval Forces Eastern Atlantic and Mediterranean (CinCNELM) was assigned additional duty as U.S. Commander Eastern Atlantic, under Commander in Chief, U.S. Atlantic Fleet. In February 1960 the further title of Commander in Chief U.S. Naval Forces Europe (CinCUSNavEur) was assigned to CinCNELM/ComEastLant. In December 1963 the title CinCNELM was disestablished and that of CinCUSNavEur remained.

Admiral Wylie: When Admiral Nimitz went out after the war, he was sent out to try and negotiate, not successfully, but it wasn't his fault. He again had more latitude than any ambassador, because an ambassador has an accreditation to a single country or in some small ones, maybe two, but not in the India-Pakistan case. He was the only fellow, short—since he'd been given his papers by the President—of the Secretary of State who could talk authoritatively to both countries. We've lost some of that. Principally, this is the great unrecognized side effect of the communications revolution. They're no longer separated by distance—instant worldwide communication. But if a naval officer finds himself in that kind of a situation such as Admiral Murfin did in 1935, he functions by virtue of his commission, as an agent of the United States, not limited as an ambassador is, to the designated country. It's probably becoming a very rare occasion now, simply by virtue of this side effect of the communications revolution.

Paul Stillwell: I'd be interested in more of your recollections of Admiral Smith.

Admiral Wylie: He's the only man I've ever known who fired a commanding officer at sea and was absolutely adamant that nobody was going to tinker with his commanding officers but him. Nobody else could put them on report. On one occasion we were doing the annual repetition of the Saipan landings down at—I guess it's Onslow Beach in North Carolina.* There was one actual Marine division, which Admiral Smith, as an amphibious group commander, had embarked. And there was one phantom division, created principally so Spike Fahrion, who was ComPhibLant at that time, would have an excuse for going.† He liked things like this. So the rehearsal was held off—it's very confusing. There are two Camp Pendletons. The one on the West Coast is substantive. The one south of Cape Henry, you know, on the coast there, is a nothing. It's called Camp Pendleton.

Anyway, we held the rehearsal there, and somebody, probably in an LSD, I don't remember, middle-sized amphibious ship, bollixed it up horribly. So Admiral Smith sent his chief of staff over to explain to this guy. We did the rehearsal again, and he didn't do

---

* This refers to the period in the early 1950s when Smith was Commander Amphibious Group Two.
† Vice Admiral Frank G. Fahrion, USN, served as Commander Amphibious Force Atlantic Fleet from January 1952 to April 1956.

quite as bad, but he bitched it. Admiral Smith shook his head, and we went on down to Onslow Beach, and he bitched it again. So he sent his chief of staff, a Captain Mewhinney, I think, over.* He gave the ship to the exec, brought the offending four-striper back to the flagship, gave him a room, and told him to stay there. Then he reported what he had done to Admiral Fahrion.

Well, Eph Holmes, with whom I was shipmates in China and very fond of, is a very careful man, and he was Admiral Fahrion's operations officer.† Captain Speck was his chief of staff.‡ You could see their fine hand. A long message came back from PhibLant that perhaps Admiral Smith a little hasty, and perhaps we'd better convene a board to check into this, so on, and so on, and so on, for about a page and a half. Admiral Smith said, "It's not necessary. I've already relieved him." And that was the end of it. Not unlike Nimitz, he was a very soft-spoken man, but if you dig beneath that, he's tougher than nails.

Mr. McNamara came through London when Admiral Smith was there, and, of course, that was during the periodic economy kicks. Mr. McNamara reportedly told Admiral Smith that he was going to take all the dependents out of Germany. Admiral Smith told him, "You'd better be ready to resign. You're not going to make it stick." And McNamara left in a huff, but he didn't dare move them, it turned out. But he was smart and tough.

I have never heard Admiral Smith talk about his time in the four-pipers in December of '41 and February of '42 in the southern islands.

Paul Stillwell: He was skipper of the <u>Stewart</u>, which fell off the keel blocks in dry dock.

Admiral Wylie: I don't know. I know he came back. I think he was in the CominCh staff—you know the difference, CominCh, CNO—for a little while.§ I don't know what he did later. But he's got that rare capacity to separate wheat from chaff. At a conference

---

* Captain Leonard S. Mewhinney, USN.
† Captain Ephraim P. Holmes, USN.
‡ Captain Robert H. Speck, USN.
§ CominCh was the abbreviation used for Commander in Chief U.S. Fleet when Admiral Ernest J. King, USN, held that title from 1941 to 1945. He was promoted to the five-star rank of fleet admiral in December 1944.

he'll let people talk as long as they want. When they're done, he homes in on the one thing that matters, and the guy may not even have known he said it, but it was crucial.

David Bruce was the ambassador I was trying to think of, quite possibly the most magnificent man I've ever known. He had the same capacity for separating wheat from chaff. Totally devoted servant of the United States, never technically a State Department employee. He was, for instance, head of the OSS in London in World War II.[*] Wealthy enough, apparently to afford it, absolutely the ablest man I've ever known.

Paul Stillwell: When you were in that job in the desflot in the late '40s, did you suffer from the short rations that the Navy was on at the time?[†]

Admiral Wylie: Wait a minute now. We've got two things. The year between my student and staff time, which would have been the year before the Korean War started, I was in desflot—chief of staff to Admiral John Higgins, who had been my squadron commodore in the last year and a half of the war. It was not that period I was talking about.

Paul Stillwell: I see.

Admiral Wylie: I had a cruiser-destroyer flotilla and a cruiser division as a young, fresh-caught flag officer in the Seventh Fleet. So I may have crossed a wire back there. It's the Seventh Fleet period I was talking about. I was not with DesFlot 1 when it was put to work after the Korean War started. I had been relieved, and I was probably in Arkansas or someplace, east-bound.

Paul Stillwell: What do you recall about that period with Higgins before you left? That was a very austere time for manning up the Seventh Fleet.

---

[*] OSS—Office of Strategic Services, formed in World War II to collect and analyze foreign intelligence and to carry out special operations under the control of the Joint Chiefs of Staff.
[†] Desflot—destroyer flotilla.

Admiral Wylie: Oh, yes. It was very often we didn't have enough men to take the destroyers to sea, or more often, we had enough to go out in the morning if we came back at night into San Diego. Nothing much was happening. Everything was churning still. The demobilization was over, but the Navy hadn't recovered. I suppose the other services hadn't recovered either from the dreadful demobilization. We were short of men and money, pathetically so, more so than in recent years.

Paul Stillwell: He had the <u>Juneau</u> as his flagship, I think, when war broke out. Is that what you were operating in?

Admiral Wylie: No. We were basically ashore, and when Rear Admiral Higgins went to sea, we went in a destroyer, not in one of the 5-inch cruisers. I think probably he was in <u>Juneau</u> at the end of World War II, because before I was detached, I guess, in July of '45 from <u>Ault</u>, about a month or two before that, he had been made a one-star commodore, and still the flotilla commander, but he wore his flag in one of the 5-inch AA cruisers, which might have been <u>Juneau</u>, I don't remember. You know, something like that.

Paul Stillwell: I'm pretty sure that was his flagship in 1950 when the war started.[*]

Admiral Wylie: He may have picked up the <u>Juneau</u> then, which would have been after I had been detached. I do not know. As I say, I was somewhere in Kansas, Arkansas, or someplace, eastbound with my family, and I heard it on the car radio.

Paul Stillwell: After you then left the war college, you got the deep-draft command in the <u>Arneb</u>. What do you recall of her?

---

[*] At the time the war began in June 1950, Rear Admiral Higgins was serving as Commander Cruiser Division Five and was embarked in the light cruiser <u>Juneau</u> (CLAA-119).

Admiral Wylie: <u>Arneb</u> was the one AKA that had been fitted for work in the Arctic.* It was a half-cock fitting. They'd strengthened the bow, they put drain cocks below all the deck saltwater risers so that when it was cold, you could drain them, and they weren't sticking out into the cold air. The hull was strengthened; it had a lot of concrete up forward and along the keel, that sort of thing. But, other than that, she was a perfectly normal KA, with, what 25, 26, 28 boats for her main battery. I was lucky. The most fun in the Navy is to put a new ship in commission—in any job, department head or captain or whatever, because you know what it turns out to be is your fault, you know.

Paul Stillwell: Or vice versa.

Admiral Wylie: That's right. And if it's a stinker, you know whose fault it is. Well, the next most fun is to take a ship which is in sad shape, because you've got no place to go but up. With all due respect to my predecessor, whose name I don't remember, <u>Arneb</u> was one of those. Don't forget, this was early '50s, and we were short on people. Right after I got there, whoever was the exec was detached, or I fired him. I don't remember. I went through three execs in five months. One of them, for instance, was a three-striper who'd never been to sea, who spent his entire Navy career—a Naval Reserve who stayed on active duty—in the welfare and recreation departments of shore stations. He came aboard, left his cap on the back of his head, blew cigar smoke in my face, and called me "Cap." You wouldn't believe it. So he didn't even get to unpack.

Finally, as I say, I went through three of them in five months, and BuPers was getting angry. And each time I filled out the paperwork and said, "This officer is totally—" What's the nice phrase that the congressmen use? There is one. I may think of it. Personally obnoxious, you know. But I finally got a proper, reasonably decent naval officer, who was a very nice man and knew his business.

That's the second time—the first time was in <u>Trever</u>—I was in a ship that required a high and specialized level of marlinspike seamanship. In destroyers, cruisers

---

* USS <u>Arneb</u> (AKA-56) was an <u>Andromeda</u>-class attack cargo ship. Originally built as a commercial cargo ship, she was acquired by the Navy and converted. She was commissioned as a Navy ship 28 April 1944. She displaced 14,200 tons, was 459 feet long, 63 feet in the beam, had a maximum draft of 26 feet, and a top speed of 16.5 knots. She had long service, including voyages to both the Arctic and Antarctic, and was eventually decommissioned 12 August 1971.

they don't, you know. But <u>Arneb</u>, with all that rigging did require it, pretty highly specialized. For instance, one day, I remembered a new second class boatswain's mate had come aboard, and I saw the leading chief boatswain's mate and said "How's Jones [or Smith, or whatever] getting on?"

To my total astonishment, the chief boatswain's mate said, "Sir, we need another couple of weeks. We haven't decided whether we're going to keep him or not."

Well, this startled me, and I finally figured it out. These guys couldn't use a battleship boatswain's mate, for instance, because if this guy wasn't good with standing and running rigging, the marlinspike seamanship, the heavy-laden boats, he'd kill somebody. And it was perfectly normal, then, for the senior chief boatswain's mate to have a veto. It took me a while to figure it out, but I did. They're a very highly specialized field.

Another illustration. Short of money, as usual, in the early '50s I was sent to the Charleston Navy Yard for a short overhaul, and the boatswain quite properly asked at the Navy yard if the ship's company could overhaul all the rigging instead of the Navy yard. They didn't trust the Navy yard. So on my worksheets for the Navy yard, I put in for the Navy yard to scrape and paint the bottom. That's usually ship's force, not a high-priced job. It just takes a hell of a lot of minimum-priced labor. I got into an absolute knock-down and drag-out with the flag officer commanding the Navy yard in Charleston. He wanted to do the rigging, which was a high-priced job, and I finally had to go to PhibLant to make it stick.

The officers were not the world's best. The main battery, as I say, was the boats. About the time I got there, I got a fresh-caught ensign from the Naval Academy, whose name eludes me at the moment. But I went out. There was a boat group commander's boat, and I went in to the beach and watched these guys straggle in in dreadful disarray on some practice landings without any troops. I tried to talk turkey to these young junior lieutenants who were putting in time. So I finally found a spot in the Navy regs to justify it, and I made this fresh-caught, bright, brisk, young Naval Academy ensign the boat group commander over all the jaygees in the boat waves, and it worked. He brought them up with a round turn. We had a lot of fun, but nothing notable.

Paul Stillwell: Where did you go on deployment?

Admiral Wylie: I was an orphan. I never worked with my own amphibious squadron. It was out of phase. I did a lot of running up to Boston and back, drove Eph Holmes crazy. He was the operations officer on the PhibLant staff. Three times I did it, filed for outside Cape Cod and went through the canal for the reason he finally figured out. If you catch the tides right, you can anchor for about four hours at the south end of the canal and get in some awfully good striper fishing. Finally, he summoned me over in the flagship and told me I couldn't do that anymore, and I agreed I'd go where I filed.

Then I was attached to Speck's squadron once for a week's maneuvers, and that made me the 12th or 13th ship to tag in.[*] On Friday we were due into New York, and we were coming up along the New Jersey coast. None of this is substantive; this is anecdotal, pure and simple.

Paul Stillwell: Sure.

Admiral Wylie: I don't know why. We were in this long column, in a dense fog, and the voice radio, then the TBS—which does not mean "talk between ships," as the newspapers say; it was the T designation for that transmitter. The previous one had probably been the TBQ or TBR. But, anyway, you could see Speck in this long accordion column behind him. They finally found Ambrose Light, and you could watch him on the radar. Speck went up north of Ambrose and anchored, and Speck's order on the TBS to his squadron, including the outsider, me, was "Proceed independently." And all the ships went up, anchored north of Ambrose Light. When I got up to Ambrose Light, that's right at the end of the channel, I took a look up there on the radar, and there was absolutely nothing. So I just said, "I don't want to do that." So I turned left and went up Ambrose Channel. I could pick up a buoy easily—you know, it's well marked—and just buoy-hop all the way up. All this time when I was going up the channel, I could hear Bob Speck counting the radar pips and trying to take a muster, you know. He had 12 anchored if I was the 13th,

---

[*] Captain Robert H. Speck, USN, served as Commander Transport Division 24 from October 1953 to December 1954.

or 11 if I was the 12th, and finally he came up and said, "Snowball Uncle, where are you?"

I said, "Passing Gravesend Bay." I don't think he ever forgave me. I got up, we got our mooring in the Navy yard, we had a nice weekend, and those guys didn't get out till Sunday morning. You know, this makes people pretty mad. But that kind of fun.

Then another time I went to New York, and at that time my family was still here in Newport, and I came up here for Saturday and went back Sunday. Monday morning we were in the Navy yard, got under way, absolutely no indication of anything unusual. We got down by Ambrose, and I told the exec, "Set the watch and start on south."

He said, "Sir, the watch is set."

I said, "What the hell are you talking about? The special sea detail was the people who had the watch overnight.

He said, "Well, sir, it just worked out, the whole ship's company had a party last night, and the only sober people on board are the people who had the duty."

I said, "My God, can't you call them out?"

He said, "No, sir, they're all drunk."

So I went on two hours south and anchored off Barnegat and went fishing. Of course, Eph Holmes heard about it. I fished until late afternoon, when, by and large, they had sobered up. It was safe to set another watch, you know. Eph summoned me again, and he said, "Goddamn it, Bill, I told you you can't do things like that."

I said, "Eph, I couldn't help it."

He said, "Why couldn't you help it?"

I said, "The whole ship's company, except for the watch up, was drunk." There wasn't anything he could say, because I didn't have another watch. But Eph and I have been friends since we were in Augusta together in the early '30s, and we understand each other.

He was my embarked flag officer when I took Macon to Chicago when they opened the seaway.[*] I don't really know that I could think of another naval officer who'd have the self-restraint not to kibitz me going up that river. He must have bitten his

---

[*] As a captain, Wylie commanded the heavy cruiser Macon (CA-132) from 29 October 1958 to 2 November 1959. Rear Admiral Ephraim P. Holmes was Commander Cruiser Division Four, 1959-60.

fingers down to the bone. I mean, this was a chancy venture, make no mistake about it. And on the second day, after we'd been in Lake St. Lambert and had the review by the Queen and the President, we started up through the next set of locks.* There's a canal leading out of Lake St. Lambert inbound. I worked from the top of the pilothouse, not on the bridge. There was a jaygee up there with a set of telephones, and it was a staff jaygee. I forget his name. I said, "What are you doing up here, son?"

He said, "Sir, I'm the FPC."

I said, "What's that?"

He said, "Sir, it's what they call me. It's the flag pacification circuit." It went down to the bridge so Eph would know what was going on. But bless his heart—I'll love him till the day I die—he never kibitzed me during or after. I don't know of any other naval officer who would have that much self-restraint.

Paul Stillwell: I've heard it said of him that if you sent over to Central Casting and asked, "Send us an admiral type," that's exactly whom you would get.

Admiral Wylie: He's a very able officer, very prudent, very careful, very orthodox, but he'll never make a big mistake, you know. Little things might get by him. I haven't got anything else.

Paul Stillwell: You've talked about that time you were in OpNav. What specifically was your billet?

Admiral Wylie: I had section 605.† Jobs gravitate in a bureaucratic organization. A lot of it depends on people. We were the firemen in my section. Jurika—I don't know whether you've encountered him or not.‡

Paul Stillwell: Yes.

---

* On 26 June 1959 President Dwight D. Eisenhower of the United States and Queen Elizabeth II of Great Britain joined in ceremonies at St. Lambert, Canada, near Montreal, that marked the official opening of the St. Lawrence Seaway, a man-made project to connect the St. Lawrence River with the Great Lakes.
† OP-605 was a subdivision of OP-06—Deputy Chief of Naval Operations (Plans and Policy).
‡ Captain Stephen Jurika, Jr., USN, whose oral history is in the Naval Institute collection.

Admiral Wylie: He was my aviator. I got an intelligence officer assigned; there had never been one in OpNav before, always up in intelligence, Fred Welden.* Hal Shear was my submarine officer, then a commander.† That was a very interesting time. Who has talked to you about the Polaris submarine?‡

Paul Stillwell: Quite a few people, but what are your recollections?

Admiral Wylie: That was the last of the major gambles that any of the services made. Admiral Burke came in, you know, quite junior, and somewhere he got the notion that this was the time to gamble. He satisfied himself that although it had never been built, a solid propellant could be put together, a nuclear-powered submarine could carry them, that you could blow these bloody things up from beneath the surface of the water, and then somebody would be there to light the fire in the tail. It was an absolutely unparalleled magnificent gamble, and the last gamble.

Well, then came the problem: once the parameters of this system had been set, how do we use them? Well, by great good luck, that fell into my section. It had the right title or something. Jurika, Hal Shear, a couple of other guys—we worked on it. What did we have—16 missiles? Absolutely silly, but there was no other way to do it. We counted the targets and counted the missiles and decided how many we'd need. Well, that isn't quite as naïve as it sounds, but it was pretty basic. We'd run the whole bloody show.

We came up with 40 submarines. About that time, mid-'50s, the Air Force was an awful lot smarter than the Navy. Instead of saying they needed 200 air wings, they said they needed either 216 or 227 or something, not a rounded number, no zeros, no fives. So we decided we didn't dare go in for 40. We'd either have to go for 41 or 39,

---

* Commander Frederick Welden, USN.
† Commander Harold E. Shear, USN. The oral history of Shear, who retired as a four-star admiral, is in the Naval Institute collection.
‡ Polaris was the name for the U.S. Navy's first submarine-launched ballistic missile, which became operational in the early 1960s.

and for a reason which I don't now recall, we went for 39 boats. Of course, that was later cut way back, but it's very interesting that 15 years later they got back to 40.*

Then came the problem of justification. I'm talking now of dollars and men, because we knew we'd have an awful job, trouble with the Air Force. We finally arrived at the conclusion, the only way we could justify this gamble is with two crews. Nobody had ever heard of two crews before. Burke saw it and looked at it. But the submariners were absolutely adamant—this was impossible. This included the senior submariner, the two-star fellow from the submarine section in OpNav, whatever it was, undersea warfare section, SubLant, and SubPac. Burke said, "Bring them around." Talking to a middle-sized four-striper? Bring him around? Hal Shear was a three-striper; Steve was a couple of years junior to me as a four-striper. Hal Shear was the first—and, for a very long time, the only—man in the Navy wearing dolphins who would publicly stand up for two crews.† Halfway through that very arduous session—it must have lasted three months—Bob Long, who, I think, was recently in the Pacific, who was in the submarine section of OpNav—he joined us and publicly spoke for it.‡

Paul Stillwell: What was the objection of having two crews?

Admiral Wylie: "It's impossible. You don't do this. You can't make it work. No reason, goddamn it. We've always done it this way." So we finally peddled the two-crew notion. Actually, it was rammed down the submariners' throats, finally, but Admiral Burke, but we held conference after conference. I did not wear dolphins, never have. Hal Shear did; later Bob Long, both three-stripers, did. We were against the whole the submarine establishment for a long time—six, seven, eight weeks—with special delegations from Norfolk and Pearl. But finally, it took—what I suspect is, Admiral Burke told them, "I can get commanders who will agree with me." I'm not sure. He

---

* USS Will Rogers (SSBN-659), the 41st and last Polaris submarine, was laid down 20 March 1965 at Electric Boat, launched 21 July 1966, and commissioned 1 April 1967.
† The insignia for a qualified submariner is a metal pin that features a pair of dolphins and a portion of a submarine.
‡ Admiral Robert L. J. Long, USN, served as Commander in Chief Pacific from 31 October 1979 to 1 July 1983. His oral history is in the Naval Institute collection.

doesn't do this in public. But that worked, and Hal Shear—we've been friends for many years—he's strong—and Long.

Paul Stillwell: He got command of one of the first Polaris boats.

Admiral Wylie: Shear had one, too, one of the first half dozen.* They're both good officers, and they're both courageous. There was literally no other way you could justify it in terms of dollars and man-hours. I don't know why the carriers don't do that today. Then they could get some fleet time in without all the trouble they're having about never being in port. It works. It's different.

Paul Stillwell: It certainly is that.

Admiral Wylie: It certainly is, but carriers would be in better material condition, too, if they'd put EDOs in as chief engineers.† Maybe they've done that now; I don't know. But get the EDOs off their fat fannies in Washington and get them in a ship. It would make or break a career—perform. Two crews per carrier? I think that would be fine.

Paul Stillwell: What do you recall from your years on the SACLant staff?‡

Admiral Wylie: I went there to retire and got struck by lightning. Yes, my record was good, but I hadn't been selected. A lot of guys are good and aren't lucky. Vice Admiral Sabin was the CinCLant deputy, and, of course, a British fellow was the SACLant deputy.§ I forget his name. He was a wild man. Admiral Sabin was on, or Admiral Dennison was president of the selection board that year—I don't know, but somehow or other, they had figured out between them that there had never been a flag officer selected

---

* When the USS Patrick Henry (SSBN-599) was commissioned on 9 April 1960, Commander Harold E. Shear, USN, was commanding officer of the blue crew, and Commander Robert L. J. Long, USN, was commanding officer of the gold crew. She was the second Polaris submarine.
† EDO—an officer designated for engineering duty only.
‡ SACLant—Supreme Allied Commander Atlantic, a naval command in the structure of the North Atlantic Treaty Organization (NATO).
§ Vice Admiral Lorenzo S. Sabin, Jr., USN. His oral history is in the Naval Institute collection.

out of the SACLant staff.* It was time there was, and that's why I got selected. Of course, that had been a retirement job for years. That's why I went there. I wouldn't go back to Washington after Macon. There was great scrambling for my job. The next guy was Elliott Loughlin; he got selected, and there hasn't been one since, as far as I know.† But it wasn't a career-enhancing job. It was fun.

I think probably the most noteworthy thing that happened in my year—well, there were two, neither of them substantive. During that year sometime, the Canadians adopted the maple leaf instead of the Union Jack. And a lot of Canadian officers on the staff, of course, so there was a big ceremony one morning at, let's say, 11:00 o'clock, hauling down the old British Canadian flag and hoisting up the maple leaf.‡ I guess naval officers are inherently conservative; this broke the hearts of all the Canadian officers there. They fought a war, you know, under the other flag, and this Liberal government up in Ottawa—well, to make the story short and succinct, everybody went into the bar, and it was sort of like that incident I described in Arneb; everybody got drunk all day long. It was just a wake. Nobody went back to their offices till the day was over, and then they didn't go back. That was a very sad occasion.

The only other noteworthy is equally frivolous. The British deputy, whose name eludes me now, vice admiral, was married to a very volatile Italian woman, who had no part in this episode I'm coming up on. But the British flag officer had himself been raised in Italy. So, you know, this was a very cosmopolitan world that they lived in. He was getting along. Anyway, he wanted to pay a visit to La Spezia, where there was some sort of an antisubmarine multinational effort going on. And I suspect, because they wanted to keep an eye on him, Admiral Sabin or Admiral Dennison sent me to go with him, along with his flag lieutenant. Whatever it was, he also had to go to a NATO

---

* Admiral Robert L. Dennison, USN, served as Supreme Allied Commander Atlantic, Commander in Chief Atlantic, and Commander in Chief Atlantic Fleet from 28 February 1960 to 30 April 1963. His oral history is in the Naval Institute collection.
† Rear Admiral Charles Elliott Loughlin, USN, whose oral history is in the Naval Institute collection.
‡ The Canadian Parliament adopted the maple leaf flag in December 1964. The incident Admiral Wylie is remembering here happened during a later tour of duty when he was on the staff of Commander in Chief Atlantic Fleet from 1964 to 1966.

conference in Lisbon with the Portuguese. They were about to create, or thinking about, IberLant then, which was a paper command.*

But, at any rate, we went to La Spezia, and then when we wanted to go over to Lisbon, we had to go to Milan to get the plane. Instead of cutting inland and taking the Autobahn up the Po Valley, this guy wanted to drive along the coast to see where he'd lived as a child. We stopped for lunch at a favorite restaurant of his. The upshot of it was that we got to Milan two hours after the plane had gone, and there wasn't another one to Lisbon for three days. The only way to get to Lisbon was to take the train to Geneva and catch a plane from Geneva the next morning. Well, he asked me, would I mind phoning Lisbon and telling them he'd be delayed. Well, I was smarter than he figured. I'd be damned if I was going to get the United States in this. This was a British effort. So the flag lieutenant did all that kind of telephoning. We got on a train late in the afternoon to go up to Geneva, no diner. We had quite literally a jug of wine, a loaf of bread, and a piece of cheese. We had more than a jug of wine.

When we got to Geneva, our heads were spinning. We found a place to sleep the night, we found the plane the next morning, the only time I've ever been to Switzerland, never saw it, except from the train station to the plane. Got over to Lisbon, and when we got to Lisbon, the delegation met him, and I said, "Admiral, you're running late. Suppose I take all the baggage, go on to the hotel," which I did, so I ducked out of that. That was an entirely British affair, but it was all right. I was sent to be a watchdog, you know. That was sort of fun, that trip, but certainly no substance.

I think it's time the NATO treaty was revised. It ends, you know, at the Tropic of Cancer, the northern tropic. NATO's interests are now worldwide. I think the treaty should be. If you follow that through, you come to a surprising answer. The principal military arm, which is a façade to support the political thing, is SACEur. If you rewrote the treaty and expanded its interests and its correlation worldwide, the principal military commander would become SACLant because of the maritime treaty. Maybe then we could get troops out of Europe.

---

* IberLant—the Iberian-Atlantic Command, a NATO command that embraced the area of Spain and Portugal.

Paul Stillwell: What do you recall of both Admiral Sabin and Admiral Dennison from that period?

Admiral Wylie: Both smarter than hell. Both very nice men, certainly kind to me. Hell, I got selected, you know, and I served 30% of my commissioned service in flag rank, 12 years.

Paul Stillwell: Which was essentially a bonus then.*

Admiral Wylie: Sure. Sure, it was. I don't know what I'd have done if I'd retired. I hadn't figured it out. The farthest I'd gotten was I figured I'd go to an employment office, and I'd tell them, "I'm a good destroyer captain. Have you got any destroyers?" You know. I didn't have any dim notion of what to do, because I still had children to educate, you see.

Paul Stillwell: You went to that cruiser-destroyer flotilla. What do you remember from that?

Admiral Wylie: Nothing exciting. Perfectly normal. I wore my flag in both Providence and Oklahoma City, both 6-inch cruisers, both converted with, I think Talos aft; I'm not sure. Terrier was the destroyer; and I think Talos was the cruiser.† Both were top-heavy; both scared the hell out of me. I'd have hated to be in a typhoon in them, enough so that I managed to get one of them scheduled for inclining experiments. I thought it was unsafe—O.K. City, I think. But that didn't take place till after I'd gone. Nothing noteworthy at all, just sort of fun.

Paul Stillwell: Then you became Deputy Inspector General. What does that individual do?

---

* Had he not been selected for rear admiral, Wylie would have had to retire at the end of 30 years of commissioned service.
† USS Oklahoma City (CLG-5) was equipped with a twin Talos launcher for surface-to-air missiles; USS Providence (CLG-6) was equipped with a twin Terrier launcher.

Admiral Wylie: Just that; he's a troubleshooter. A classmate of mine was the Inspector General. There were problems with the Antarctic, and he didn't want to become involved in it, and so I was sent down to the Antarctic. Well, you do some homework before you go, and it was pretty evident before we left, a party of about four, that the problem wasn't down at McMurdo Sound; it was in Washington. But it also became evident somebody had to go to McMurdo Sound to prove it. These were supply problems, dull, logistic stuff. I thoroughly enjoyed it. I'd obviously never been there. You go to Christchurch. Then you take a plane 2,000 miles to McMurdo Sound; 1,000 miles out is the point of no return. It gets to be pretty cold, you know. They were just starting to build, but had not completed, the atomic power reactor at McMurdo Sound. David Tyree—there were two Tyree flag officers, one David and one John, and I think David was the elder, and they're not related, no kin at all.

Paul Stillwell: David is the one the mountain's named for in Antarctica.[*]

Admiral Wylie: That's the one. Well, David was the one down there, one of the nicest men you ever knew. It didn't take long for my people to get whatever it was they needed to prove the trouble was in Washington. You know what I mean, the Bureau of Something or other. While I was there, two interesting things. I went up to the Pole one day, caught a ride on one of those great big four-engine propeller things on skis—C-47, whatever. What most people don't realize, and I certainly didn't, the altitude is 10,000 feet, the air is thin, the temperature when I got there was 40 below. There's a very fast turn-around up there of people out, cargo out, people in, because they don't dare turn off the engines. Because if they turn off the engines, they have to erect these canvas huts and put heaters in them before they can start them again.

Anyway, the first noteworthy incident, maybe about 100 yards away from the airplane when we got out was a flagpole, and that's the South Pole. So we trudged over in god-awful heavy clothes and boots on, all issued before we left Christchurch. We finally got over there, huffing and puffing, 10,000 feet, rare air, very cold, and I walked

---

[*] Rear Admiral David M. Tyree, USN, Commander Naval Support Force Antarctica, 1959-63.

around the world, twice, and suddenly was overcome with the most dreadful depression. All I could think of was, "Wylie, what in God's name are you doing at the South Pole?" Just an encompassing depression: "This is wrong, you know." Finally, we went down below the surface—they live all under snow there—and warmed up a little bit and gradually regained my senses, but for half an hour it's the most dreadful psychic disarray I've ever been in. I can't explain it. Maybe it happens to other people. But the mere fact of being at the South Pole was just psychically devastating. Interesting.

The other notable event was at McMurdo Sound. They had been planning for some time to open another station over towards the Weddell Peninsula under South America. Now, what they planned to do was send in a light DC-3, whatever the service designation of that is, on skis, to take some gear in and a small tractor to smooth the runway in the ruffled snow for the big—is it the C-47, or is that a DC-3?[*]

Paul Stillwell: I think that's a DC-3.

Admiral Wylie: These were C-54s or something.[†] So the big four-engine plane on skis could get in, and, of course, the major problem was weather. Can they do both these event? The reason it was a problem was, they start for McMurdo Sound, straight south is the South Pole; angled off to the left is Byrd Station, 600-800 miles apart, and then another 600 or 800 miles past Byrd Station is where they wanted to go down toward the base of the peninsula. Of course, the key man in this is the weatherman. And for three mornings I went to the briefing and watched this weatherman. I was an observer, not a participant. I suddenly realized what this guy was trying to do was sit in New York with a friend in Chicago and a friend in Atlanta, forecasting Phoenix. And they made it. They finally got it. It was one of the most interesting operational planning things I've ever seen.

One other thing. We're in our anecdotage. I went over one day to—I guess it's Reutz, near McMurdo Sound, the place where a brand of penguins have their roosts. It's

---

[*] The DC-3 was as superb as a cargo or passenger plane; in World War II the DC-3 carried the Navy designation of R4D and the Army Air Forces designation C-47.
[†] R5D Skymaster was the Navy designation for the Douglas-built DC-4 commercial airliner. The Air Force Designation was C-54.

gravel, mostly stones, about golf-ball size or a little smaller, just shingle, and it's bare. The penguins were there by the thousands. The system is that the gentleman penguin picks up one of these little stones, and he lays it at the feet of another penguin. If it turns and walks away, it's either another gentleman or a bespoke lady, so he tries it again. Finally, somebody will pick it up, and that's the acceptance, and they go off, and they build a very shallow depression, and put the eggs in it, and sit on the thing.

Well, before I left, a contemporary of mine, a classmate, Counihan, had said, "I hear you're going to the Antarctic."*

I said, "Yes."

He said, "Bring me something."

I said, "All right." Well, the exchange at McMurdo Sound was in a closet and consisted mostly of tiepins made in Providence or something, you know. So I didn't do that, but I got a handful of these little stones, golf-ball size or smaller. When I came back, I took one down to Counihan's office, and he wasn't there. He had a little cross-eyed secretary, and she said she didn't know when he'd be back. I said, "Would you give him a message?" So she got her shorthand book, and she was juggling this rock in her hand, and I explained all this to her. And I said, "I have a friend from New Zealand who's also taking some home. He's going to take them to dinner parties, and he's going to put one of those stones down in front of his dinner partner, and he said, 'God help her if she picks it up.'"

And she went "Ooh!" and threw it across the room.

About three or four hours later, Counihan phoned and said, "There's a rock here, and she won't tell me anything about it."

But it was very interesting. They're fearless. You can walk right in among them.

Paul Stillwell: If you ever have designs on a female penguin, you're all set."

Admiral Wylie: Yep. That funny little girl was just so shocked. She'd been tossing this stone up in her left hand while she shorthanded.

I made one very major decision. I did not touch the magnet that draws men back.

---

* Captain John L. Counihan, Jr., USN.

Paul Stillwell: And you've never been there since.

Admiral Wylie: I've been there. Boy, that's it. I don't understand these people that winter over. Bleak and cold.

Paul Stillwell: Unfortunately, I must make my exit at this point.

Admiral Wylie: Well, obviously, I've run out.

Paul Stillwell: Then that's perfect timing.

Admiral Wylie: I wish you well.

Paul Stillwell: Thank you, I have enjoyed it. I think one of the principal appeals of this is listening to the stories and anecdotes.

Admiral Wylie: It's almost a catharsis, isn't it, when you invited somebody to unload?

Paul Stillwell: Yes.

Admiral Wylie: We were talking before we started here, how much of it is self-interest—an awful lot of it in this session, not blatant, but egocentric, surely.

Paul Stillwell: I don't know necessarily. They are things that you were involved in. You didn't paint yourself as a hero.

Admiral Wylie: I can't think of anything else useful that I can contribute if, in fact, any of it has been.

Paul Stillwell: I think it is, and the rest, really, will come perhaps years from now when somebody digs this up.

Admiral Wylie: We'll never know, will we? It won't happen on my watch. It might not happen on yours.

J.C.Wylie
627 Black Point Lane
Portsmouth, R.I. 02871
21 May, 1984

Dear Peter,

On one of my infrequent spurts of "cleaning out" things that have accumulated over the years, I came upon this chart of the waters off Guadalcanal. With some nostalgia, I considered throwing it away when another thought came to mind.

I realized that if, sixty or more years ago, I had had whatever maps or notes or documents that my own grandfather had had at Gettysburg (he was, I believe, a captain in Company "F" of the Sixth South Carolina Volunteers which at Gettysburg served in Pickett's Division of Longstreet's Corps), this would have been of interest to me. That war was then not much more than half a century behind me. And, in only eight years from this time, the battles of Guadalcanal will be just half a century back from your time.

So here is the chart I used as Executive Officer and Navigator of the destroyer Fletcher off Guadalcanal in the autumn of 1942. Obviously, it has been repeatedly used and erased and no single action or track now shows on it. There were several major and minor anti-aircraft actions in protection of the ships delivering men and supplies to the Marines ashore; there were casual bombardments of the Japanese troops, initially west of the Tenaru River and more often near the Matanikau River; and there were two major actions on the 13th and 30th of November.

The 13th of November, which was the first of three days of what was later termed the naval Battle of Guadalcanal, was described by that best of historians, S.E.Morison, as "the most desperate sea fight since Flamborough Head" (when John Paul Jones and his crew captured the British Serapis while his own Bon Homme Richard sank alongside).

In case superstition intrigues you, I'd better tell you about that Friday the thirteenth. The ship was named after one Frank Friday Fletcher (I think the father of the Admiral Commanding at the Battle of the Coral Sea earlier that same autumn of 1942). The action took place on Friday the 13th of November. Fletcher's hull number was 445, and she was sailing that night in Task Force 67. Fletcher was the 13th ship in a column of 13. There were 5 five-inch and 8 40-mm guns. The middle of the night at Guadalcanal must have been close to 1300 Greenwich time. And you may be sure that, after the action, the ship's company found a lot more things that added up to thirteen. Fletcher was the only U.S.ship of those thirteen that was not sunk or damaged.

Of particular interest was the fact that Fletcher was one of only two of those thirteen ships that had the then-brand-new SG radar. This was the first appearance of the PPI, Plan Position Indicator, a polar presentation radar screen. All prior radars had had only a radial presentation (an A-scope) which meant you could see echoes only in the direction in which the antenna was aimed at any moment. With the polar PPI presentation, you could see everything, all 360 degrees, to whatever radial range the radar was set.

We had SG radar serial number 3, so you can see that it was new. The only other SG radar that night was in our sister destroyer O"Bannon.

We, in Fletcher, had tried to explain to the two flag officers present (Callaghan and Scott) by visual message the day before that we had this PPI presentation radar which gave us vastly more and better information than anything in the other ships. There was no response. Since this was so radically new an idea, I guess they did not take it aboard. It was beyond their psychological infinity. This is the sort of a mental block that you may come up against at the most unexpected times; be ready for it. All you can do when you recognize that you've encountered it is to be patient, and start all over again by the numbers. It is a most frustrating situation.

Let me illustrate: the evening before the action we were milling around in Indispensable Strait, probably lying to a little northwest of Nura Island. I was sitting on the radar in the chart house just abaft the bridge, watching (on the radar) the transports and stores ships coming east out of Sealark and Lengo Channels after unloading, and others headed northwest up Indispensable Strait getting in position to take more supplies in to the Marines the next morning. I noticed in particular one ship coming east and one headed northwest on tracks that would intersect three or four miles north of Nura Island. The voice radio (then called the TBS which was the letter designator of that particular transmitter) was full of chatter and it was not too difficult to identify the voice calls of those two ships.

So I called each of them on the radio and told them they were each on a collision course with the other. Neither altered course and I suppose they thought I was some kind of an unauthorized nut. At any rate, they did collide. Apparently it was not serious, but collide they did. And no other ship or commander had the perspicacity to ask how we forecast that collision on a pitch black stormy night with no ships showing lights.

There had been information, probably from the coast-watchers (those true and unnoted heroes), that a Japanese force was headed for Guadalcanal to bombard the Marines and their airfield that night (the coast-watchers were planters who had been in the Solomons and volunteered to take a couple of natives and go up in the hills overlooking the Jap bases and radio to our people what they saw; many of them were found and killed). So Admiral Callaghan collected a pick-up team, formed a column of four destroyers, five cruisers, and then four more destroyers, and stood in to what was already called Ironbottom Bay from the large numbers of ships sunk there that autumn. There was then no formal name for that water but it has since been called Savo Sound, the water between Guadalcanal and Florida and Savo Islands.

I think we entered through Lengo Channel but my memory is not sure on all of these details. When clear of the Channel, the leading ship was ordered to head northwesterly (the last coherent order of the night) and we all followed in succession, Fletcher at the tail of the long column. It was a night as black as only a stormy tropic night can be.

The Nips came in from close past Savo Island, and our own leading destroyer, blind, steamed right into the middle of the Jap formation. It was an incredible melee.

At one point Barton, a destroyer just ahead of us, blew up and disintegrated. A gun or torpedo shot must have found and touched off a magazine. Some of the debris landed on our decks but no one was injured from that. I don't recall that more than a dozen of her survivors were found and picked up the next morning by boats from Guadalcanal.

I can not consciously remember why, but I made a series of pencil sketches of the radar screen during the action, showing both our own ships and the Nips. At one time I counted radar pips totalling 26 ships including our own (I think it later turned out there were 15 Japs, so I missed a couple) all of them inside a circle whose diameter was about two miles and most of them in the middle of that mess. I suspect that not since Trafalgar had there been so many ships fighting in so small an area, and I am not at all sure that the longer lines at Trafalfar did not spread those ships to a lesser density than in Ironbottom Bay that night.

Like all the others, we were firing every gun we had at point blank range, including the 20mm machine guns. Of course, in the chart house where the radar was, I did not see this, but my captain on the bridge called in to tell me it was just like fourth of July. At one point he called in to tell me "Aren't you glad our wives don't know where we are tonight!"

To go back a bit: when we had gone through the Panama Canal westbound in late August or early September, we had somehow mooched from the U.S.Army in Panama (for a case of whiskey, perhaps) four more 20mm machine guns. Our shipfitters jury-rigged some mounts for these guns on the main deck in the waist of the ship. One of the young signalman strikers was assigned as a loader to the gun on the starboard side about abreast the mainmast.

Piecing together the stories later (which was my job as Exec), a Japanese destroyer about 100 yards on our starboard beam had fired at least four torpedoes at us. Our crew could see this, not only the flare of the torpedo impulse charges launching them, but the ships themselves in the flare of the guns and burning ships. Of course, and fortunately, the range was too short and I doubt that the arming mechanisms had functioned. Certainly the torpedoes had not found their steady running depth. One porpoised on the surface close astern, two went under our ship, and one porpoised on the surface close under the bow.

Well, our little signalman striker on the after 20mm saw a torpedo headed straight for him. He took off, as fast as he could run, heading for "home" which for him was the signal bridge. He ran forward half the length of the ship, up three decks on those steep ladders, and over to the port side. He looked over the bridge bulwark and, behold, he saw a torpedo emerging and going away. Nothing, then or later, could convince him that he had not run all that distance forward and up three decks and across to the port side in the time it took that torpedo to dive under the ship and come up close to the port side going away. A world speed record. What he had seen, of course, was one torpedo aft starting to dive, and another forward, fired later, emerging from under the ship. But he would never believe this. I doubt that he does even today. At any rate, this is a sample of why the crew went to every length searching out the obviously lucky thirteens.

Soon after that, the captain on the bridge spotted a Japanese cruiser, too close for our torpedoes to arm, so the captain identified that ship for me on the radar (bearing and range) and he made a big circle to the southeast so that we had perhaps 1500 yards for our notoriously lousy torpedoes to seek proper depth and arm the exploders. From the radar I coached the torpedo director on to the target and we let go all ten of them. After the torpedoes had been fired, and our watches were ticking off the running time, I ran out on the bridge to watch, too. There were flares at the correct time and I am sure, today, that we got a couple of hits. But the post-war battle analysis did not confirm this.

How anyone could "analyze" that wild chaos I will never know.

To illustrate: during the action I made pencil sketches of the radar scope. When we got back to Espiritu Santo a few days later, I used those sketches to write the ship's Action Report for my captain to sign and send in (it was the Exec's job to do this). Lying there at anchor in Segund Channel, I had just reviewed the typed copy when Doc McDonald came by in a boat to take me ashore to cadge a drink from the Seabees building an airstrip. He was Exec of O"Bannon, the only other ship with an SG radar. He was discouraged because he could not piece together a coherent account for his Action Report. He had been on the bridge, not on the radar in the chart house as I had been. So I said "Look, Doc, here are my sketches, and at the beginning when we were still in column, here is O"Bannon as the second ship in the column. All you have to do is re-draw these sketches with O"Bannon in the center and send them in". He made some hasty sketches and we went ashore and found some beer.

Six or eight months later, in Pearl Harbor, my curiosity took me to the Historical Section of the CinCPacFlt Staff and I asked about the battle of the 13th of November. "Oh, that was easy" the historian said, " two of the ships had SG PPI radars and they both sent in sketches. There were some discrepancies, of course, but O"Bannon was up near the head of the column and wherever there were disagreements we used O"Bannon's sketches because she was closer early in the action". Thus is history graven in stone.

The next morning we were working our way out of Indispensable Strait to the southeastward and set course for Espiritu Santo. O"Bannon, whose sonar had been put out of action by the explosion of a near-by ship, had been sent north of Malaita Island to transmit by radio the action summary of the C.O. Helena, the senior survivor. Helena was the guide ship. San Francisco, very badly battered, was astern of her (under command of a classmate, Bruce McCandless, since the admiral and captain and exec had all been killed) with her main deck nearly awash aft. Portland, I think, was astern of her moderately damaged, and Juneau was off on the starboard quarter of SanFrancisco and roughly astern of Fletcher. Juneau had been badly hit and earlier that morning Helena had sent some welders over by boat to help restore Juneau's watertight integrity. Helena's damage was not serious. The destroyer Sterrett, I think it was, with her sonar gear inoperative and much other damage, was out on Helena's port bow burying her dead. Fletcher, undamaged, was on Helena's starboard bow pinging away in a normal anti-submarine search. There may have been a third destroyer out ahead but I do not recall.

My captain, Bill Cole, and I were in the chart house just aft of the bridge. We had asked the ship's doctor to bring us a gill of medicinal whiskey and we had just poured it into two glasses.

Then there was a terrific explosion somewhere. We never did get to drink the whiskey.

We ran out on to the bridge and looked aft. Juneau, almost a mile astern of us, had simply disintegrated and the air was full of pieces. I don't remember which of us did which, I think it was he who got on the public address system and passed the word for all hands to take cover, and I rang up emergency flank speed on the engine order telegraph. One of Juneau's twin 5-inch gun mounts landed less than a hundred yards from us directly in our wake.

We thought a welder's torch had touched off a magazine, and so turned hard right to go back and look for survivors, though I do not, to this day, see how any human could have survived that explosion

We had turned almost 180 degrees when we got a peremptory order to resume our anti-submarine screening station. Of course we were sore as hell. But a little later Captain Gil Hoover in Helena sent us an explanatory visual message. He had had reports of at least two Japanese submarines somewhere along our track and, more importantly, Helena had seen the torpedo cross between Helena and SanFrancisco and, by chance, go on to hit Juneau and touch off one or more magazines.

In retrospect, I think that decision of Captain Hoover's was probably the most difficult decision I have ever seen an officer make. Every instinct tells us to go after possible survivors, but he knew, and we did not, that there was an immediate submarine hazard. Helena was the only cruiser in the South Pacific anywhere near combat-ready, and he had the very badly damaged SanFrancisco and at least two other cripples in company. Those were his over-riding responsibilities. It must have hurt like the devil to call us off the search for survivors, but he had the courage to do it without hesitation.

Juneau, by the way, was the ship in which the five Sullivan brothers were lost. Not long after that, Washington sent out orders to disperse close relatives to forestall more family calamities of that sort. Later a ship was named The Sullivans.

Rear Admiral Callaghan, lost in SanFrancisco, was posthumously awarded a Medal of Honor. I think if he had survived, a court martial would have been almost inevitable. He had another flag officer, Rear Admiral Scott in Atlanta (he was killed), he had a destroyer squadron commander in, I think, AaronWard, and may have had a destroyer division commander in one of the four destroyers toward the head of that column. No unit commanders were given any ships or tasks. Nor were any individual ships. The disparate types of ships were just formed in one long column and the last coherent order was a northwesterly course. The destroyers could have been used in one or two groups befitting their capabilities, and even Admiral Scott could have been put in the act with the two anti-aircraft cruisers and their large 5-inch gun batteries. In my opinion, it was incredibly stupid not to use the destroyers under command as one or two separate units. Instead, we reverted to a time before Trafalgar and put every one in one long unmanageable column. Just plain stupid.

Then, two weeeks later, on November 30th, there was another action, conducted with equal incompetence by another flag officer named Wright (not the Jerry Wright who after the war became CincLantFlt) . He had good information that Jap destroyers were coming down the Slot with supplies that night. He had five cruisers and four destroyers. My Captain, Bill Cole, was the senior destroyer officer. Wright formed a column of four destroyers, five cruisers, then at the last minute two more destroyers he picked up going into Ironbottom Bay. We were specifically instructed by visual signal before dark not to open fire until ordered. Which is a cue as to how dumb that bastard was.

Again it was dark. Fletcher followed by three destroyers leading the column, followed by five cruisers, and then two last-minute destroyers who never got any orders or information at all about anything.

Just a little beyond the Matinikau River, about four miles offshore and headed parallel to the shore, I spotted several radar pips coming in fast from Cape Esperance and close in to the beach. Obviously they were the destroyers we were looking for. I gave the bearing and range and course and speed of the Nips to the other destroyers (we had the only SG radar) and then asked Admiral Wright for permission to fire torpedoes. He said "Negative". To quote Sam Morison " The squadron commander in Fletcher with good radar asked permission for his four van destroyers to fire torpedoes; Wright hesitated for four minutes before granting it, and so lost the battle".

That gave time for the Nips to see us, to fire their own much better torpedoes, and to turn around and get away. By the time our own torpedoes were fired, the Jap torpedoes were already in the water. Three of our cruisers had their bows blown off and a fourth sank later that night. (As an aside, I do not know of any other destroyer or any destroyer officers other than those of us in Fletcher who fired a total of twenty torpedoes in anger during the entire war).

The fifth cruiser in the column was Honolulu with Rear Admiral Mahlon Tisdale embarked. Junior to Wright, he had played no part until he saw the four cruisers ahead of him all hit. Then he sheared out to the right and came roaring up wide open. He asked what the Nips were doing, realizing that we had a good radar(sitting at the radar I also had the voice radio) and I told him the Nips were headed home. He said "Get cracking" and he and the four destroyers set out after the Japs. Our pitometer log registered 37 knots, an impossible speed for those ships, but we could not catch them. After perhaps 15 or 20 minutes of futile pursuit he turned us around and told two of us to go back to pick up survivors.

By that time, three damaged cruisers were working thir way over to some kind of shelter at Tulagi, and Northampton was burning furiously where she had been torpedoed and stopped an hour or more earlier.

A couple of months previously, we in Fletcher had recognized that, if we survived, we would sooner or later have to pick up large numbers of survivors from other ships. And we had only the one whaleboat. So we had prepared by rigging two 100-fathom lengths of light 21-thread line and stopped off pieces of torn up life jackets at intervals along these two lines to make sure they would float.

As we neared Northampton, we could see hundreds of men in the water and the oil. Bill Cole conned; I went aft. He backed the ship in toward the masses of men in the water. I made sure the boat officer knew that he was to pick up no one other than those seriously injured and in danger of immediate drowning. So the whaleboat took one end of one 100-fathom line and made a large swing around men in the water. Then he brought his end of the line back to the fantail where we had rigged cargo nets for the survivors to climb. While our men on deck were hauling in that large bight of line, and sweeping survivors to the cargo nets, the whaleboat took the other line and bagged another batch of men.

The other destroyer picked up, I think, 72 survivors. We picked up 708. Or maybe the figures were 78 and 702.

Counting our own ship's company, we had about 1000 men on board, enough to give us a stability problem if all of them were topside and much of our fuel expended. So we let our survivors topside in relays. The galley, augmented by cooks from Northampton, operated 24 hours round the clock. Most of their oily clothing was thrown overboard and our crew and small stores refitted the survivors with clean clothing.

At daylight, with an air raid warning from Guadalcanal, we went out Lengo Channel and headed for Espiritu Santo. The three damaged cruisers had worked their way over to Tulagi and I think that is where Admiral Tisdale went to look after them. I don't know where the other destroyers went.

We later learned that Wright had flown to SoPac headquarters in Noumea and blamed the debacle on us, and on Cole in particular, for not staying with the cruisers en route Tulagi. Cole was relieved of his command. Only later did ComSoPac acknowledge his error and made Cole "ComDesSoPac", but he had lost his ship command.

There were some hasty and ill-considered judgments after these two dreadfully managed actions of the 13th and 30th. Captain Hoover had been relieved for not picking up survivors from Juneau (he was correct and courageous in what he did), and Bill Cole was relieved after picking up an impossible 700-plus survivors. Of course when the full story was known some days later, that dumb bastard Wright was sent ashore for the duration. He should have been courtmartialled.

In late December, I was ordered to command Trever, a dirty old WWI four-piper converted to a three-stack DMS, a destroyer minesweeper. After a short stay in the naval field hospital outside Noumea to have my hemorrhoids repaired (a lousy job, too) I took Trever. Within a week we had a minesweeping assignment, I forget where. Getting underway that morning, we had hove in to short stay when the engineer called up the voice tube that one of the two engines was out of order. I acknowledged, then ordered the forecastle to heave right up. About the time the anchor was in sight, the engineer came roaring up to the bridge, very angry, to shout at me (the newcomer to the ship) that he had only one shaft and that he could not answer bells. I said as long as he had one shaft he damned well could, and rang up one third ahead. He went tearing back to his engine room. We swept, as scheduled, on one shaft. And, in the six months I had Trever, we never had another engineering casualty.

On one occasion early in that winter of 1943, Jack Tennant and I (he was a classmate who had another DMS, and was later killed by a stray shell, I think at Tarawa) (or it could have been Pete Wirtz in '31 who had Zane) were taking a number of Army troops up to one of the little known islands up the Slot from Guadalcanal. A rubber boat landing. The 18th and 19th century charts were quite inaccurate, but we did have current aerial photos clearly showing a break in the coral reef large enough for our ships to enter and close the island itself.

In the dark of night we could not find the break in the reef. So we fell back on our only chance. We tried to find the hole by braille, easing forward until the bow touched then backing off and trying again. Eventually one or the other of us found the hole and we both went inside the reef. Our embarked troops were part of a National Guard Division just arrived in the South Pacific. We, the two ships' captains, knew but the soldiers did not know that there were no Japs on the island. It was sort of a test for them.

I should have smelled a mouse because, on the way up the slot at dusk, there was an unusual exchange of semaphore messages between my senior troop officer, a lieutenant colonel, and his boss, a colonel, in the other ship. Whatever was the substance of the mesage, I questioned it and my embarked light colonel replied " Oh, don't worry about that. I am the game warden back home and he is my chief poacher. We understand each other from 'way back". Odd. At any rate, we found the landing location and inflated the rubber boats and the men started ashore. After a while, when the debarkation should have been completed, the Chief Boatswain's Mate came to the bridge and said, "Sir, them senior officers don't want to go ashore". So I went down to the main deck and explained that if they did not climb down into those boats my men would throw them in. They went. The other DMS captain had essentially the same problem in his ship.

When we got back to Guadalcanal, we two captains went ashore to the Amphibious Group Headquarters to report two matters to the Chief of Staff, an elderly Captain Doyle ("elderly", you understand, is always a relative term).

He listened to our tales of the National Guard officers and said nothing then, but that entire division was put into reserve, re-officered, retrained, and later did very well in the northern Solomons around Bougainville. There must have been other incidents, too, to have brought forth such quick and drastic action.

Next, we told him that we had grounded our ships looking for the hole in the reef and he kept interrupting us, talking about other and irrelevant things. We both thought he had slipped into his rambling dotage. Finally, he indicated that the visit was over and we got up to go. As we got to the door or the tent flap, whichever it was, he said "By the way, I understand there may be problems with the underwater transmitters on your echo ranging anti-submarine gear. I'll see that you get divers to inspect them".

What that dear old man had done was to prevent us from telling him that we had committed the cardinal sin of grounding our ships. The last-minute casual comment about divers was his way of letting us find and fix any damage to our bows without anything on the record. There may have been some dummies among our seniors early in the war, but there were lots more who were just fine.

On another occasion while in Trever, I was summoned ashore to Camp Alligator, the Amphibious H.Q., on Guadalcanal. It was explained to me that a Marine reconnaissance party was to make a wide sweep around the Japanese, a trip of several days, and that they were expected to reach the shore just beyond Cape Esperance on, say, a Tuesday. I was to meet them there and replenish their food and ammunition after their week or so in the jungle. The orders were a little vague, it was not positive they would make it on Tuesday, so I should also be there on Monday and Wednesday, and, while the Marines had set the rendezvous time at 0100, I had better be there by 2300 and wait till 0400 on each night. As I was leaving, I asked who was the Marine officer in charge of the recon unit. The answer was "a Major Puller".

I had sailed for about four years with Louis Puller in Augusta in the early 'thirties and knew him well.

So I got cocky and said "Oh, I know him, Captain Doyle, and if he said 0100 Tuesday he'll be there then. No sense my losing sleep on Monday. I'll take the boat in myself to meet him at 0100 Tuesday". And made my manners and departed. I am sure dear Captain Doyle was too flabbergasted to say anything.

So on Tuesday I took two or three bottles of whiskey and went myself with his replenishment food and ammunition and met Louis Puller on schedule. We had a drink or two while the boat was being unloaded, I left the whiskey with him for his troops, he thanked me, we wished each other well, and I shoved off. The last I heard at that meeting was his terse order to his men: "Move out!".

And now I am going to digress. In about 1934, in Manila, Louis Puller, then a First Lieutenant of Marines, was training his troops (the ship's Marine Guard) while the ship was running through the entire annual gunnery schedule in order not to interfere with the activities of the Commander-in-Chief Asiatic Fleet during the rest of the year.

I walked into the wardroom one evening after dinner and Puller and Lloyd Mustin (a classmate) were in a heated argument. Lloyd maintained that a man had to be born with certain skills in order to shoot a rifle or a pistol well. Puller's position was the opposite. As I came in he was declaiming "I can teach any dumb bastard to shoot". As I neared he pointed and said "I can even teach him". The bet was ten dollars.

So the next week I went off with Louis and his Marines to Camp McKinley outside Manila and for two weeks I shot that nine-pound Springfield '03 rifle. On the last day of the two weeks I shot for record, starting at 500 yards prone and finishing at 100 yards offhand (with no sling). I earned a Marine Expert Rifleman medal with points to spare. Louis won his ten dollars. And I have included that Marine Expert ribbon on my uniforms ever since. It is my Louis Puller medal.

And one more Louis Puller story. When I had Arneb in the early 1950's, an amphibious cargo ship (AKA), I was to take some Marines from Camp Lejeune (Moorhead City) to Vieques. Puller had already had a stroke but was still the Commanding General at Lejeune. It had, typically, always been his custom to visit his embarking marines in the ships just prior to sailing.

I was visited in Norfolk by two officers from his staff. They explained that, since the accomodation ladders on AKAs were so long and steep, they were not going to let the general go on board, and would I please come ashore to greet him on the pierside at Moorhead City when he came to say goodbye to his troops. I said I understood the situation.

So I rigged a special cargo pallet with lifelines, bolted an armchair in the center, rigged a canopy overhead, and when the general's cavalcade drove up swung the chair overside and down on the pier alongside the general's car. As Louis got out of the car, a seaman planted a three star flag on the corner of the pallet, Louis stepped on and sat, and he was whisked up on deck where his departing troops were lined up waiting.

After he spoke to his men, we went into my cabin for coffee (laced with a bit of rum for the occasion) and talked about this and that. Then back on deck and he sat again in the special chair on the pallet. As the strain came on the running rigging and he rose in the air to go back ashore, he said "Thanks, Bill". And I am sure that the toughest Marine of all had tears in his eyes. His pallet was put down near the waiting car, he drove off and never looked back. But he had seen his troops off on board ship as he had always done.

I have other Puller stories, too, but that is enough for now.

Love, Grandfather

J. C. WYLIE
627 BLACK POINT LANE
PORTSMOUTH, R. I. 02871

8 October, 1984

Dear Peter,

A couple of weeks ago I was in Annapolis attending a reunion of the crew of the USS AULT (DD698) which was my second command during World War II. This destroyer was built at the Federal Shipbuilding and Drydock Company at Kearney, N.J. (I was the commissioning C.O.) and was commissioned at the Brooklyn Navy Yard on (I think) 31 May, 1944. The AULT reunion group is almost unique among ship reunions in that it limits itself to those who served in World War II; it does not include those many who served in her only after that war. This was the reunion to mark the 40th anniversary of the commissioning. There were 66 men plus many of their wives at the reunion.

I found the weekend both interesting and fun --- fun because obviously it consisted principally of reminiscences and interesting because I soon realized that this group was a cross-section of America. When one considers that, in 1944, the ship's company was made up of a mix of volunteers and draftees (mostly the latter I suppose) from all walks of life, and that most of the crew was between the ages of 17 and 20, it really was a random cross section of the population. And last week the group contained everything from retired construction workers, postal rural delivery men, telephone line stringers, to bank presidents (one), and financial entrepreneurs (one, details not known). Raucous most of the time, bawdy, and nearly all of them had bathed their year and a half in AULT at war in an aura of great excitement and good times.

One of my particular friends was the ship's baker, a man named Bob Scales. The bakers used to bake at night in order to leave the galley clear for the cooks doing their three meals a day plus snacks any time. In the forward areas of the Western Pacific I used to get up about 3:00 am, shave and shower, and then go down to the galley to get fresh hot bread for breakfast and be done with all that before the usual General Quarters at morning light. When I saw Scales at the reunion, he asked me if I remembered the 5-gallon stainless steel cooking kettle he kept in the corner of the galley. When I said "No", he explained that that was his raisin mash. He kept it fermenting for his friends the whole time. Somehow he had the notion that I knew about it and purposely overlooked it, so I tried to stay non-committal in spite of my surprise. Such are the knacks and oddities of leadership and command. I suppose he figured I was a 4.0 fellow because I let him keep his brew fermenting. And I guess he still thinks so.

It is some of the more normal reminiscences that I propose to tell you about in this letter. Since I was asked to speak after the Saturday evening dinner, I asked what they wanted me to talk about. They said three things: (1) the neutrality patrol in 1941 (AULT was not involved in this), (2) the AULT and our tour in the Third and Fifth Fleets from the Luzon Invasion to Okinawa, and (3) the planning for the prospective invasions of Kyushu and Honshu which were scheduled to take place after Okinawa. So, in this letter, I shall touch upon all three of these with some items additional to those I mentioned at the dinner.

In 1941 I sailed in USS BRISTOL, one of the broken-deck (i.e. raised forecastle) destroyers, built at Federal Shipbuilding and Drydock Co. in Kearney, N.J., and commissioned in the Brooklyn Navy Yard in the summer of 1941. I was, I think, torpedo officer, but principally I was one of the deck watch officers.

The first thing I told the AULT crew at the dinner was that there was nothing neutral about the Neutrality Patrol before the U.S. officially entered the war. In September of 1941 the GREER, a destroyer, mixed with what later turned out to have been U-652 and depth charges and torpedoes were fired. All missed. On 17 October the destroyer KEARNEY was torpedoed and lost 11 men, but the ship made port. On October 30th, the oiler SALINAS was torpedoed but made port. The next day the old World War I destroyer REUBEN JAMES was torpedoed and sunk with a loss of 115 officers and men. I lost a good friend in her wardroom.

In the autumn of 1941, we escorted convoys to MOMP (Mid-Ocean Meeting Point) and there turned the convoys over to British escorts. After the US entered the war officially after December 7th, we went with convoys all the way to Londonderry.

In mid-December BRISTOL and two other destroyers were sent to a mid-ocean rendezvous amid great secrecy. Our captain did not even tell his wardroom what for. Then one morning out of the mist came the KING GEORGE V (or one of the other British battleships of this class), making 25 knots into gale force winds and a very rough sea. One destroyer took station right ahead, one on the port bow, and BRISTOL on the starboard bow. In that rough weather and at that speed we were no use at all as anti-submarine escorts. It was all we could do to hang on. We took too much green water in the port whaleboat, it cracked open and the two halves hung each at its own davit head. A devil of a job to cut that mess loose. The destroyer right ahead of KG V had not properly secured his anchor chain and the pelican hook let go. To make things worse, the bitter end was shackled in the chain locker (I never have let the bitter end be shackled; always had it made fast with line so it would part in event of such a mishap). So this poor fellow found himself in a high wind and sea and more than a hundred fathoms of chain and anchor hanging down. He had to stop and KG V passed him close aboard at speed. How he got out of his predicament I do not know. We were never in company again.

At any rate, we arrived in Norfolk, anchored where we were told, and relaxed to catch our breath. That evening after dark, a US battleship came into Hampton Roads, anchored, and sent us a peremptory message: "You are fouling my anchorage. Move". We had to get up steam and move at midnight. But I did get ashore to phone your grandmother and she got a train and we had Christmas together in Norfolk. We also learned from the newspapers that Winston Churchill had arrived in Washington , so at last we knew who we were escorting in that vile weather across the western half of the Atlantic.

It must have been about February of 1942 that BRISTOL was part of a mixed escort taking a convoy from Halifax to Londonderry. My captain was the senior and thus the escort commodore. There were a couple of Canadian corvettes plus a Free French corvette (Gaullist, not Vichy French) and a corvette manned by Poles. Those corvettes were even more uncomfortable in the North Atlantic than was our gold-plated destroyer (the destroyers built in the 'thirties were called gold-plated in contrast to the World War I four-pipers that the Navy had been using for nearly twenty years). In BRISTOL the oficers rooms were all well forward and we could not stay in our bunks to sleep when it was rough. The bow would rise rapidly, toss the occupant in the air, then move sideways and let the occupant thump down on the deck. We solved the sleeping problem by welding some billet hooks on the wardroom bulkheads and rigging hammocks which do not toss you out. It must have been even worse for the corvettes, all built in Britain but, in the cases of the French and the Poles, manned by refugees who had escaped the Nazi invaders.

Our captain, taking his ship on a turn around the convoy one evening at dusk, sent over to the Frenchman a courteous "Comment ca va?". The answer was a long and laboured apology, in English, that he had been having steering problems but would try and do better in the future. Odd. When we arrived in Londonderry, we found out that he had a British signalman on board who had received the message as "Comment. CA VA". He then looked up CA and VA in the merchant signal book and found that they meant "you are off station, explain why" or some such, which was the message he gave to the French captain. Hence the unexpected and rather pathetic answer.

We also learned that, on arrival in Londonderry, the French had on board two prisoners whom they proudly presented to the British. They were the Vichy Governor of St. Pierre and Miquelon, two little islands south of Newfoundland which were all the French were allowed to retain after the Seven Years War in the mid-eighteenth century. The other prisoner was the Governor's wife.

The British, for some inscrutable reason, would not accept the prisoners. What happened to them? I do not know. When the Free French corvette had taken them, St. Pierre and Miquelon shifted sides and became Free French. Like the story of the Lady and the Tiger, the outcome is unknown.

The Polish corvette was a different matter. I asked one of our British friends in Londonderry what they were doing in the Atlantic since the ships manned by Poles were normally assigned to escort and aircraft rescue duties in the North Sea off the east coast of England. It seems that this corvette had come upon a downed German airplane in the North Sea, had closed to investigate, seen the survivors in the water, and shot them.

The British, back in port, explained to the Poles that this was not cricket. One only shot people like that after they had been court-martialled.

So the next time this Polish corvette came upon a downed German aircraft, they took the survivors on board, held a court-martial on deck, found them guilty, shot them, and threw them back.

The British decided that drastic action was in order, so they sentenced the Polish corvette to two round trips in trans-Atlantic convoy duty.

In Argentia, Newfoundland, for fueling in March or April of 1942 I received despatch orders for fitting out and commissioning the FLETCHER as Exec.. I have previously written you about a few of my experiences in her, in the South Pacific. With these orders in hand, I went by local train from Argentia to St.Johns and there took the narrow gauge sleeper train across that large island to Port Aux Basques. During the night crossing the hills in the middle of the island, I looked out and saw near the tracks in the moonlight a herd of moose or caribou. I've never known which but it was most impressive.

On arrival at Port Aux Basques, I took the ferry across Cabot Strait to Sydney Mines on Cape Breton Island, Nova Scotia. There I took a train to New York. I travelled about 1500 miles by train, mostly westward, and ended up in New York. The next night, the ferry was torpedoed in Cabot Strait.

Now for the second topic ---- AULT and the western Pacific.

AULT was the fourth new ship in eight years in which I was part of the fitting out and commissioning detail from the Federal Yard in Kearney. REID, BRISTOL, FLETCHER, and now AULT, this time as Commanding Officer. Most of the men I had known as workmen when the first three were being built were now foremen. The result was that I was able to get a lot of refinements and goodies in AULT that none of the other ships had. For instance, voice tubes: These were usually installed with right angle joints wherever the voice tubing changed direction. In AULT, there was never a bend of less than three-foot radius. The result was that the voice-pipes worked; the clarity was perfect, no muffled garbles. Little things like that.

One result was that our squadron commander who went with each ship of his squadron to Bermuda for shakedown, made that trip in AULT. We were so much better equipped than the others that he stayed in AULT rather than his assigned flagship until late July of 1945 when he made one star and shifted his flag to a 5-inch AA cruiser.

One of the problems of putting a new ship in commission is that of creating an identity for the crew. By that time all the destroyers had Coca Cola machines and even, beginning with our squadron, ice cream machines. How to make AULT unique? How to give the crew something to talk about that set it apart from the other destroyers?

So, before the ship was delivered to the Brooklyn Navy Yard, I called on the District Attorney of Essex County in Newark. I asked him to give me a couple of nickel slot machines. He looked startled and said "Of course I can't give you any slot machines; what do you want them for?". I explained. He thought a moment and said "I can't give you any slot machines, but I can give you a couple of devices to illustrate the evils of gambling". Slot machines were then mechanical, not electronic, and he had all the stops taken out of the cog wheels to rig them for maximum pay-off, and we took them to Kearney and locked them in one of the ship's magazines.

When we left Pearl Harbor, westbound, early that autumn of 1944, I had them set up in the crew's messing space and organized a three-man committee of chief petty officers to count the money and put it in the paymasters safe. You wouldn't believe how busy those machines were, and how much money they raked in. So, I think in November, I sent a storekeeper with all the money back to Pearl Harbor in an oiler. At the various Ship's Stores (now called Navy Exchanges) at the DesBase, the SubBase, the Navy Yard, etc. he bought enough presents for every man in the ship and got another oiler back to the fleet. A small committee on board AULT gift-wrapped all the presents and numbered each one. Some had cost a dollar, others as much as twenty-five dollars. Then, at Christmas dinner, each person drew a number out of a hat and, after dinner, picked up his correspondingly numbered present. I am sure it was the only ship west of Pearl Harbor in which every officer and man had a Christmas present.

Gradually, during the winter and spring of 1945, the avid enchantment with the slot machines began to fade, but they had served their purpose. The crew bragged about them and, regrettably, wrote home about them.

I began to get mail. One father, an irate Minister of the Gospel, wrote of his indignation about everything from gambling and morals to subversion of the war effort when people at home were on rations. He also wrote the same thing to the newspapers, which the wire services picked up, and to the Secretary of the Navy.

The first two letters from the Office of His Lordship the Secretary I threw away.

Then, in late spring, nested with other destroyers in Ulithi Atoll, I noticed large numbers of men from the other ships coming on board. Our crew was inviting them so they would feed the slots and make money. After a couple of days of this, I was visited by my fellow skippers from the other ships, a delegation, who thought it would be a good idea to share the proceeds of our slots with them. I told them to bug off. Why didn't they go see a district attorney when they were next in the United States?

But on that same day I got my third letter from the Secretary, and it was a little more tart. So I figured the two slot machines had served their purpose and sent them over to the enlisted beer-grounds on one of the sand-spit islands of that atoll; its name really was Mog Mog Island. Then I wrote the Secretary saying that I had transported the two slot machines to the Western Pacific for the enlisted club ashore, and suggested that the Secretary might choose to write to the Naval Advanced Base Commander on Mog Mog, Ulithi Atoll.

I doubt that he did.

Small bit of one-upsmanship: the standard reward for picking up downed pilots and returning them to their carrier had, for years, been a gallon of ice cream. We were the first squadron of destroyers with our own ice cream machines. So, taking back the first pilot we fished out of the drink, the carrier sent the usual short semaphore message "Ice cream?" So we sent back "What flavor would you like?" A collateral result of that was that the reward for a downed pilot became a quart of Schenley's Black Label. By any measure that was absolutely the worst whiskey ever made. The wardroom would not drink it, the chief petty officers were polite but made awful faces, so I sent most of that over to Mog Mog too.

Our squadron, 62 I think, deployed as a squadron, a relative rarity, and stayed together in the same fast carrier task group screen through the rest of the war. I think it was the only squadron with consecutive hull numbers (696 through 704, nine ships).

When we passed through Pearl Harbor westbound, I had noticed that the taxicabs had radios, the then-new FM radios. So we bought one for each ship and rigged 12 volt power supplies on the bridges. All our intra-squadron communications were on that private circuit and we were, to an outsider, the quietest squadron in the fleet. With three squadrons in the screen, the other fellows never knew how we talked to each other and, by tacit common consent, we never told anyone. Those early short-range FM sets were marvellous. Everyone thought we did everything by doctrine and never had to talk on the radio. It made our commodore look good, too.

I had a cat in AULT. I like animal company but think it cruel to take a dog aboard ship because they can not be broken to a sand box and someone has to clean up. But cats are easy, and every ship has a sand locker. So my cat Maggie lived with me in the sea cabin and got along fine with the bridge crew, sleeping on the flag bags in good sunny weather.

Two incidents.

One night, during the first air raids on Tokyo, it was cold and wet and I had my sea boots ready beside the bunk in the sea cabin. I was called during the night, swung myself out of the bunk and into the boots, and started out to the bridge. But Maggie was already in one of the warm boots. Hard to tell which of us was more surprised and annoyed, and I had trouble getting the boot off. The watch on the bridge was in hysterics. Only later did I see what was funny. And was teased about it for weeks.

Periodically, and normally, Maggie came into season. She would then climb up above the bridge into the Meccano-like fire control radar atop the gun director where she would sing and call all night. All the ships had, by then, been equipped with infra-red visual signalling devices, and one night the signalmen sent out a call for volunteers. The next morning they showed me some of the replies from other ships volunteering the services of cats, dogs, monkeys, parrots, and so on from all over the fleet. I did not see our own outgoing message, but I suspect it was a bit bawdy.

Since I was detached at sea in July of 1945, I learned only last weekend that Maggie jumped ship when AULT finally arrived in San Francisco after the war. Everyone else was being frantically demobilized so I guess she followed suit.

During these first raids on Tokyo by the fast carrier task force (which preceded the more publicized raids by the B-29s from Tinian and Saipan), the Navy put about 1500 planes over Tokyo in addition to the fighter defenses retained for the five carrier task groups. Quite possibly, in numbers of aircraft, this was the biggest single air attack in all of World War II. Of course, when an air raid is sent in from the sea, one of the hazards is having the enemy planes follow your own returning aircraft to find out where the launching ships are.

To counter that procedure, we had several pairs of destroyers 50 miles or more out to the side and our own returning planes came to them, flew low around the "de-lousing" destroyers for a good visual inspection, and then after they had been de-loused vectoring the planes back to their own carriers. It worked.

Because I had Commodore Higgins embarked (he was the senior squadron commander of the three in the screen and thus the screen commander) I never was assigned picket duty 20 or 30 miles out from the heavy ships. This was where destroyers got hurt. So I took all the night plane guard duty.

The operation off Okinawa was the first appearance of specially trained night air groups. They were embarked in light carriers (CVL) built on cruiser hulls. With both attack and fighter planes, they flew only at night. And flying at night was then a very chancy business.

We devised a pilot pick-up system which worked well (this was before the time of helicopters, destroyers did all this pilot rescue work). The lowest point of the main deck was amidships, so we rigged a cargo net there to use as a ladder as well as a jigger to hoist a wire stretcher for the injured who could not climb. From that point in the waist of the ship we ran lines forward to the forecastle outside the life lines. One of these had an outsize floating monkey fist which was thrown down to the men in the water as soon as I could lay the bow of the ship close enough. The second line was attached to a harness on a swimmer ready on the forecastle. The third (and fourth if there were two men in the water) were attached by snaphooks to the swimmer's harness. He went overboard as soon as we were close enough and snapped the extra line or lines under the armpits of the men in the water. Then all lines were hauled in to the waist of the ship.

The first time we tried this the swimmer (a boatswain mate named John Simon who was at the reunion) watched the pilot struggle to climb the cargo net with his heavy, waterlogged parachute on his back. The pilot would not take off his parachute. After arguing with Simon, he started up the net again and of course could not make it. So Simon took out his knife and cut the webbing straps, freed the parachute, and the pilot climbed up on deck. After that we put another man on a line and harness in the water at the cargo net. He had a sharp knife, and as the pilot started up, he cut the parachute loose without any comment.

Pilots learn early in their training that a parachute means survival. When in trouble and under psychic tension they will not discard it, no matter what. Which is why we cut it off without comment as soon as they started to climb. The scenario on deck was always the same. A big breath of relief, a few sheepish grins, and then a sudden and furious "Who stole my parachute?" At this point, someone would hand him his parachute, dripping. Again he would look sheepish, say "thanks", and give it away to the nearest seaman.

As far as I know, we never missed one who got out of his plane before it sank. Most of the hundred-odd pilots I picked up during the war were directly off carriers, deck landing mishaps. But some in damaged planes made water landings. In these cases a destroyer (often AULT because I liked this) steamed clear of the formation and the pilot made his water landing ahead of us where we could reach him quickly. Same rescue swimmer system. As a sort of an aside, during World War II, in BRISTOL, FLETCHER, and AULT I was involved in picking over a thousand men out of the water one way or another. Of these, seven hundred plus were the survivors of NORTHAMPTON that I told you about in a prior letter. A few were in the North Atlantic, too. But over a thousand all told.

Other destroyer skippers of course had their own systems. Mine was reliable and quick. I liked it. It worked.

Plane guarding the CVL at night, we had an extra voice radio tuned to the carrier landing frequency, so we could usually anticipate a job coming up. Sometimes a pilot knew and reported what was wrong. Just as often, we could sense from his voice pattern that he was a prospect for trouble in the landing. Tenseness and anxiety seemed to come through if you listened for it carefully. Remember that night flying is normal now; then it was a very dangerous novelty and the only aid a pilot had in landing on a darkened ship deck was the lighted wands of the Landing Signal Officer on his platform back on the port quarter of the flight deck. More than once those LSOs had to step back off their platforms and fall into the safety net below in order to get out of the way of an errant plane who came in a little left of where he should have.

Normally as destroyer plane guard I steamed about 200 or 300 yards and 30 degrees off the starboard quarter of the carrier, well clear of the landing pattern. When we sensed trouble, I took the conn and closed up to about 50 or 75 yards where we could go hard left and then hard right to run up the port side of the carrier wake to the plane in the water. Usually, by the time we had the rudder back to the right I was already backing the shafts to get the way off.

Illustration: One night a fighter plane had been hit and the radio was out. Another plane picked him up and led the way back to the carrier. What the pilot of the crippled plane did not know was that he had also lost his wheels and his tail hook, which the escort reported by radio to the carrier. So the carrier knew it and we knew it. But the pilot of the crippled plane did not and , at night, there was no way to tell him by hand signals. So the CVL cleared its decks and told the escort plane to lead the cripple into the landing circle. Of course he ran the length of the deck and over the port bow. We got him OK.

Next morning when we were closing the CVL to high-line him back to his carrier, he came to the bridge (as they all did) to say thanks. I asked him if he had known that he had more than radio trouble and he said, "No, sir, but when I landed and saw the island go by I knew I was in trouble". Those brave young men were marvellous beyond description.

Another pilot rescue story. The second strike launch of the day was usually about eight o'clock after which the dawn launch was retrieved. One fighter pilot of this 8:00 am launch from one of the Essex-class carriers was soon shot up over Okinawa and just did manage to coax his plane as far as the water, but not very far from the Japanese-held beaches.

We kept a submarine a little way off shore to rescue pilots in this situation, but in this case the pilot was too close in and the water too shoal for the submarine to pick him up. So a float plane which had been catapulted from a battleship or a cruiser, for bombardment spotting, made a water landing and taxied to the downed pilot. With two already in the plane, there was no room inside and the rescued pilot hung on the float while the plane taxied out to the submarine. The submarine then took him out to a battleship on a trip to collect his mail. After the morning launch, AULT had volunteered to take mail from our offshore carrier operating area in to the bombardment group simply because I wanted a look at what was going on ashore on Okinawa. The downed pilot was high-lined to AULT from the battleship. When I got back to the carrier group, I transferred him back to his carrier. When he got out of the high-line chair on the carrier deck, he turned to wave and fell flat on his face.

What had happened was simple. Rescued pilots were always given a gill of medicinal whiskey. He got 4 oz. of whiskey in the submarine; 4 more ounces in the battleship; and the usual 4 ounces in AULT. He had been launched at 8 o'clock, been shot down, made a water landing, ridden the floats of a float plane, been transferred to a submarine, then to a battleship, then to a destroyer, then back to his own carrier before the rest of his launch had been recovered (all in about 2 hours), and had 12 ounces of whiskey in his tummy. He passed out and we later learned that he slept more than 24 hours until lunchtime the next day.

Off Okinawa, each of the five fast carrier task groups normally consisted of four or five Essex class CV, plus one CVL for the night air group. Each group also had one or two of the new fast battleships, 2, 3, or 4 of the 6" or 8" cruisers plus one of the 5" AA cruisers, plus three squadrons of destroyers (25 to 27 DD) in the circular screen. Five such groups made up the fast carrier task force. This surely must have been the most powerful armada that ever put to sea. In additon there were the hordes of all sizes and kinds of amphibious ships and the large numbers of all kinds of logistic support ships to furnish the food, fuel, ammunition, and replacement planes. We seldom saw the amphibious and logistic support ships except when we dropped back a hundred miles or more to replenish.

Destroyers topped off fuel about every other day from the carriers, battleships and cruisers in company. Every five or six days an entire group would drop back a hundred and fifty miles or so for a dawn rendezvous with a logistic support group, each of which included a hospital ship.

Which brings up another story. When BUNKER HILL (CV) was hit by a kamikaze, there were serious and persistent fires in her hangar deck. I followed her for about four hours, picking up men who had been forced overboard off the stern by the flames and smoke. I don't recall precisely, but I think we picked up 60 to 80 survivors.

Some of them were injured, so that night I went to the rear area and made a dawn rendezvous with one of the hospital ships. We were transferring injured in stretchers and others by boatswain's chair on high lines at 15 knots. I usually put AULT about 60 feet on these personnel transfers and with a good helmsman this was no problem. (On fuel and food and ammunition I worked at about 100 feet, easier on the helmsman).

On this occasion the helmsman reported a little difficulty in holding course, and I realized we had about a 7-degree list to port, toward the hospital ship. Querying the chief engineer he stoutly maintained, his pride wounded, that all liquids (fuel and water) were properly disposed and balanced. I looked aft over the bridge bulwark and there was the problem. Every man not on watch was at the port rail goggling up at a nurse on the upper deck much higher than our ship, who was sitting in a chair reading a magazine with her feet up on the upper rail. That bitchy vixen was putting on a show. Finally one of our signalmen got off the long glass and asked permission to use the loud hailer. I nodded, he picked up the microphone, aimed the hailer, and said: "Hey, babe, your magazine is upside down". Which it apparently was. She fled. Our men eventually left the port railings and we got rid of our list to port.

But we had an unexpected follow-on. For the next several days fights broke out all over the ship for no apparent reasons. After a couple of days the Exec, Vince Healy, and I finally figured it out. We had on board well over a couple of hundred men whose average age was 18 to 20. A man-of-war is basically a very artificial microcosm of society, and a society under abnormal tensions. A fairly high level of discomfort, odd hours, always an underlay of trepidation, generally prevailing tiredness if not exhaustion, rigorous demands of performance, and then suddenly added to this was an awareness absent for many months. They were behaving just like the mountain goats butting their heads together in the rutting season. We had a shipload of young studs, and, when this unexpected new tension was added by that bitchy nurse, they just fought with each other for no reason other than instinct. It took about a month for these otherwise senseless fights to die out. I don't know who she was, but she sure caused a lot of trouble that I did not need at that time.

Altogether, in the Okinawa campaign, AULT steamed for 91 days without stopping the shafts. Those 600-pound steam plants were marvellous. I suspect this sort of durability has been exceeded only in the last couple of years by the ships in the Indian Ocean south of the Middle Eastern area, and they did not have the almost continual 4-boiler steaming and the frequent if not prevailing needs for 25 knots or better most of the time.

We had a couple of typhoons during that campaign, too. Then and now I fault the Third Fleet Commander for failure to recognize bad weather and lousy seamanship. During the worst of one of them, we were heading not only into the seas but into the worse part of the hurricane. So I told my Commodore (embarked) I was leaving the formation to care for my ship. He agreed and I so informed the task group commander and turned away to a safer course. Several of the

page 12

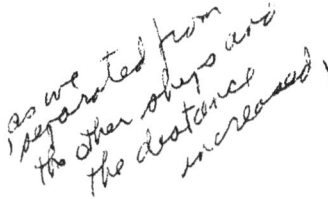
(as we separated from the other ships and the distance increased)

other destroyers then did likewise. One of the last voice radio transmissions I heard was the voice of Rivets Rivero who was Exec of the cruiser PITTSBURGH, saying to the ships astern of him, "Our bow just floated down our port side".

As for the third item the men wanted discussed at the 1984 AULT reunion ----- the invasion planning for Kyushu and Honshu ----- I could offer little. My commodore was involved on the fringes of this, and at one time he said that the Navy and the Army Air Force had each submitted requirements for radio frequencies which, each, exceeded the number in the frequency spectrum then available. It would have been a communications nightmare.

Of more importance, the best preliminary estimate of casualties was around 50%, in ships, in crews, in embarked troops, in troops ashore. I suppose half of us then in the fleet would not have survived the war if we had had to lay on those invasions. I, for one, am very glad indeed that we dropped those two bombs, one on Hiroshima and one on Nagasaki. I honestly believe that there would have been more U.S. casualties if we had had to invade than there were casualties in those two cities, to say nothing of the Japanese casualties if there had been an invasion. This is not to say that I favor the use of atomic weapons today, that is another and far more complex matter, but I am very glad they were used against the Japs who started that war and the bombs ended it.

I was detached from AULT some time in July of 1944 and ordered to Washington to serve in the newly created Special Defense Section of the ComInch office. Two explanations: ComInch (Commander in Chief) was the title chosen by Admiral Ernie King when he got the CNO job soon after the seventh of December 1941. He separated the administration from the operational control of the Navy and his Deputy CNO ran the former. Admiral King was the operating chief. This was in acordance with the law then existing. Only the head of the Navy was the operating head of his service. Not the Army or the Army Air Force , their head was literally "Chief of Staff"of the Army. Anyway, the acronym for the Commander in Chief of the US Fleet had previously been "CinCUS", and King would have none of that since the Japs had recently complied with much of it. So he changed the title to COMINCH. And second explanation: the then Commodore Arleigh Burke had been ordered to Washington to figure out how to handle the kamikazi business so he had gotten ordered to his section one officer from just about every kind of naval warfare, one battleship officer, one fighter plane officer, one amphibious officer, etc. I was the destroyer officer. I think there were about ten or twelve of us. The war ended before we really did any good.

When the war ended, of course our reason for being in that job disappeared. At the time I felt strongly (still do) about the schism between sailors and aviators , so I went over to BuPers with two offers. I would go back to sea as Exec of a carrier (a job then and now reserved for aviators) or I would go back to sea in a destroyer if I could have as my exec a carrier aviator who had had no ship duty and was going to stay in the Navy. Of course the aviator detailers would have none of this sort of heresy, so I looked around for a hole to crawl into for the coming chaos of demobilization. I found one in the Office of Naval Research, and there I stayed until 1948. Then I abolished my job and got ordered to the War College.

Enough now, for recollections. Fortunately, at my age, I conform to the normal human tendency to forget the bad things and remember only the good, the pleasant, the humorous, the human side of the story. I pray that you never have to fight a war.

With much love,

Index to the Oral History of
Rear Admiral Joseph C. Wylie, Jr.
U.S. Navy (Retired)

Aircraft Carriers
Destroyers rescued downed carrier pilots in the Pacific in 1944-45, 52-54

Air Force, U.S.
In the early 1950s Air Force officers were guest speakers at the Naval War College, 89; was not in position to respond during the Suez crisis in the autumn of 1956, 66; role in the spring of 1965 during a U.S. intervention in the Dominican Republic in response to a rebellion there, 63-64

Alcohol
In the late 1920s, Naval Academy midshipmen found ways to get drinks, 4, 12; around 1930 an instructor in the Naval Academy ordnance department showed up drunk when he was supposed to teach a class, 11; in the Orient in the mid-1930s Scotch was even cheaper than beer, 17; in late 1934 the Lord Mayor of Melbourne, Australia, found a sly way to provide grog for the officers of the heavy cruiser Augusta (CA-31), 31; in early 1943 the pilfering of beer by a crew member of the destroyer minesweeper Trever (DMS-16) was handled by an unofficial disciplinary system, 44-45; the crew of the attack cargo ship Arneb (AKA-56) had trouble operating the ship one morning in the early 1950s when many were drunk, 103

Altair, USS (AD-11)
Old, slow tender that in the late 1930s served destroyers in the San Diego area, 46-47

Ammunition
In 1942 the crew of the destroyer Fletcher (DD-445) had to remedy defective flashless powder charges, 58-59

Amphibious Warfare
As Commander Amphibious Group Two in the mid-1950s, Rear Admiral Harold Page Smith gave a speech on amphibious warfare to the NATO Defense College, 90; in the mid-1950s Atlantic Fleet ships conducted a practice landing at Onslow Beach, North Carolina, 96-97

Antarctica
In the early 1960s, as the Navy's Deputy Inspector General, Wylie went to Antarctica to demonstrate that problems concerning that area were really problems in Washington, 111-112; establishment of a station near the Weddell Peninsula, 112; activities of penguins, 112-113

Arctic
    In the summer of 1931 the research submarine Nautilus tried unsuccessfully to go under the arctic icecap and had to be towed to port by the battleship Wyoming (BB-32), 14; the attack cargo ship Arneb (AKA-56) was strengthened for operations in the early 1950s in the arctic ice, 100

Army, U.S.
    Was not in position to respond during the Suez crisis in the autumn of 1956, 66-67; role in the spring of 1965 during a U.S. intervention in the Dominican Republic in response to a rebellion there, 64

Arneb, USS (AKA-56)
    Was strengthened for operations in the early 1950s in the arctic ice, 100; had some substandard officers, 100; requirement for a specialized type of boatswain's mate to handle boats and rigging, 100-101; overhaul in Charleston, 101; boat group operations, 101; visits to ports on the East Coast in the early 1950s, 102-103; the crew had trouble operating the ship one morning when many were drunk, 103

Asiatic Fleet, U.S.
    In the mid-1930s, as fleet flagship, the heavy cruiser Augusta (CA-31) visited a number of ports in the Far East, 16, 24-25, 30-32, 94-95; in the 1930s the crew of the Augusta included some enlisted personnel who were of the breed known as "Asiatic sailors," 24-25; role of the fleet commander in chief in 1935 as a diplomat, 94-95

Atlantic Fleet, U.S.
    Role of the fleet staff in the spring of 1965, when the Navy had ships stationed off the Dominican Republic during a time of unrest and eventually sent Marines into the country to maintain order, 61-65

Augusta, USS (CA-31)
    Operations in the early 1930s off the West Coast, 15; the ship's first three commanding officers, in the early 1930s, were top-notch leaders who eventually reached high rank, 17-20; in 1933 had a yard period at the Puget Sound Navy Yard, 19-20; training of junior officers, 21; the ship was in Long Beach, California, at the time of the March 1933 earthquake and provided relief measures for civilians ashore, 21-22; service in the mid-1930s in the Orient as flagship for Commander in Chief Asiatic Fleet, 16, 24-25, 30-32, 94-95; in the 1930s the crew included some enlisted personnel who were of the breed known as "Asiatic sailors," 24-26; First Lieutenant Lewis Puller was part of the ship's Marine detachment, 27-28, 31-32; in late 1934 the ship paid a visit to Melbourne, Australia, 30-32; in late 1935 the ship visited several ports, including Bangkok, 94-95

Ault, USS (DD-698)
    Did shakedown training around Bermuda in 1944, 54-55; in the autumn of 1944, when Wylie took the ship through Pearl Harbor, he called on Admiral Chester

Nimitz, Commander in Chief Pacific Fleet, 18-19; in 1944-45 the ship rescued dozens of downed naval aviators in the Pacific, 52-54

Australia
In late 1934 the heavy cruiser Augusta (CA-31) paid a visit to Melbourne, 30-32

Bangkok, Siam
In late 1935, as Commander in Chief U.S. Asiatic Fleet, Admiral Orin G. Murfin performed diplomatic service in Bangkok, 94-96

Beakley, Rear Admiral Wallace M., USN (USNA, 1924)
In the early 1950s, as deputy to the president of the Naval War College, changed the duties of a group that was studying the role of the Navy, 91

Begg, Admiral Sir Varyl C., Royal Navy
As Britain's First Sea Lord in the mid-1960s, got help from the U.S. Navy in stimulating support in Parliament, 79

Bristol, USS (DD-453)
After being commissioned in October 1941, this destroyer went into convoy escort duty in the North Atlantic, 47-51

Brown, Vice Admiral Charles R., USN (USNA, 1921)
Role as Commander Sixth Fleet in the autumn of 1956, during the Suez crisis, 67-68

Bruce, David K. E.
Outstanding individual who served throughout the 1960s as U.S. Ambassador to Great Britain, 80-81, 98

Burdick, Lieutenant Commander Eugene L., USNR
Naval Reserve officer who in the early 1950s, while at the Naval War College, was involved in writing a study on the reasons for the existence of the Navy, 87; in the mid-1960s proposed a follow-up to the earlier study but died in 1965 before it could be accomplished, 91-92

Bureau of Ordnance
Problems in World War II with unreliable weapons, particularly torpedoes, 58-60

Burke, Admiral Arleigh A., USN (USNA, 1923)
In 1945 collected a number of officers to seek countermeasures against Japanese suicide planes, 22-23, 33; as Chief of Naval Operations had an active role in the mid-1950s in the Polaris ballistic missile submarine program, 105-107; as CNO acted energetically in response to the Suez crisis of 1956 and the Lebanon crisis of 1958, 65-70, 83-84; gave the okay in 1956 for establishment of an OpNav operations center, 83-84; leadership style as CNO in working with officers on the OpNav staff, 82-83

Cabot, USS (CVL-28)
 In the spring of 1945 operated as part of Task Group 58.3 during combat operations against the Japanese, 54

Caldwell, Rear Admiral Henry Howard, USN (USNA, 1927)
 In the spring of 1965, as Commandant of the Tenth Naval District, ordered naval forces to the vicinity of the Dominican Republic during a crisis there, 63

Canada
 In 1959 the heavy cruiser Macon (CA-132) transited the newly opened St. Lawrence Seaway and visited Chicago, 103-104; reaction of Canadian officers at Norfolk in 1964 when Canada adopted the maple leaf flag, 108

Carney, Commander Robert B., USN (USNA, 1916)
 In 1936-37 served as first commanding officer of the destroyer Reid (DD-369), 42-43

Chamoun, Camille
 Lebanese President during the U.S. Marine landings in that nation in the summer of 1958, 68-69

Charleston Naval Shipyard
 In the early 1950s overhauled the attack cargo ship Arneb (AKA-56), 101

Chehab, General Fouad
 Lebanese Army commander during the U.S. Marine landings in Lebanon in the summer of 1958, 68-69

China
 In the mid-1930s, the heavy cruiser Augusta (CA-31), flagship of the U.S. Asiatic Fleet, visited various Chinese ports, 16, 24-25

Cole, Commander William M., USN (USNA, 1924)
 In 1942 was commanding officer of the destroyer Fletcher (DD-445) during her shakedown training in the Caribbean, 56-57; in December 1942, under his command, the Fletcher rescued hundreds of crew members from the heavy cruiser Northampton (CA-26) near Guadalcanal, 52-53, 55-56

Combat Information Center Doctrine
 In 1943, under the leadership of Rear Admiral Mahlon Tisdale, the Destroyer Force Pacific Fleet worked on developing shipboard CIC doctrine, 36-40, 85

Commercial Aircraft
 In the mid-1930s the first Pan American clipper flying boat arrived in Manila, Philippine Islands, 93-94

Commercial Ships
  In March 1967 the Liberian-flag tanker Torrey Canyon went aground off England and created a large oil spill, 79-80

Communism
  In 1933, two junior officers from the heavy cruiser Augusta (CA-31) encountered Communist recruiters while in Seattle, 19-20

Conolly, Vice Admiral Richard L., USN (USNA, 1914)
  As president of the Naval War College in the early 1950s, encouraged a study on the reasons for the existence of the Navy, 87-88, 91

Constantine II, King
  In the spring of 1967, at the time of a coup by Greek military officers, the U.S. Navy made plans for possible evacuation of the monarch from Greece, 73

Constitution, USS (Wood-hulled Frigate)
  In the early 1970s anti-Vietnam War protesters chained themselves to the ship's mast, but Marines dealt with the situation in a way that minimized publicity, 34

Convoys
  In 1941-42 the destroyer Bristol (DD-453) escorted convoys in the North Atlantic, 48-51; in the fall of 1942 the destroyer Fletcher (DD-445) escorted convoys in the vicinity of Trinidad, 56-57

Counihan, Captain John L., USN (USNA, 1932)
  In the early 1960s, while serving in Washington, asked for and received a souvenir of Wylie's trip to Antarctica, 113

Depth Charges
  In World War II, U.S. depth charges had an unpredictable sinking rate until the British teardrop shape was adopted, 59

Destroyer Flotilla One
  Had few operations during the period on the West Coast in 1949-50, 98-99

Destroyer Force, Atlantic Fleet
  In 1943 worked in tandem with its Pacific counterpart in getting changes made in destroyers, 40

Destroyer Force, Pacific Fleet
  In 1943, under the leadership of Rear Admiral Mahlon Tisdale, the type command worked on developing shipboard combat information center doctrine and teaching destroyer practices to untrained crews, 36-40

Destroyers
In the late 1930s, many of the inactive four-stackers laid up in San Diego had been cannibalized to provide parts for other ships, 46-47; in 1943, under the leadership of Rear Admiral Mahlon Tisdale, the Destroyer Force Pacific Fleet worked on developing shipboard CIC doctrine, 36-40, 85; destroyers rescued downed carrier pilots in the Pacific in 1944-45, 52-54

Deyo, Rear Admiral Morton L., USN (USNA, 1911)
As ComDesLant in 1943, worked in tandem with his Pacific counterpart in recommending changes in destroyer design, 40

Disciplinary Matters
Handling of problems in the mid-1930s on board the heavy cruiser Augusta (CA-31), 24-26; in the early 1970s Marine drug dealers were moved out of Portsmouth Naval Prison to keep them away from anti-Vietnam War demonstrators, 34-35

Dominican Republic
In the spring of 1965 the Navy had ships stationed off the Dominican Republic during a time of rebellion and eventually sent Marines into the country to maintain order, 61-65; role of the U.S. Army and Air Force in the 1965 intervention, 63-64

Doyle, Captain James H., Jr., USN (USNA, 1920)
In early 1943, while on the staff of Rear Admiral Richmond K. Turner, directed the destroyer minesweeper Trever (DMS-16) to resupply Marines on Guadalcanal, 29

Egypt
Response of the U.S. Navy in the fall of 1956 after President Gamal Nasser nationalized the Suez Canal and U.S. allies sent military forces to the area, 65-68, in June 1967 Israeli forces attacked and badly damaged the U.S. intelligence ship Liberty (AGTR-5) near the Sinai peninsula, 74-77

Eisenhower, President Dwight D.
Role in the autumn of 1956 during the Suez crisis, 66-67; during the Lebanon landings in the summer of 1958, 68

Enlisted Personnel
In the 1930s the crew of the heavy cruiser Augusta (CA-31) included some enlisted personnel who were of the breed known as "Asiatic sailors," 24-26; many of the talented enlisted men of the 1930s Navy were officers in World War II, 26; when the destroyer Fletcher (DD-445) was commissioned in the summer of 1942, the crew contained three illiterates, 57-58

F-5L (Flying Boat)
In the summer of 1930 was used for aviation indoctrination training for Naval Academy midshipmen, 13

Fahrion, Vice Admiral Frank G., USN (USNA, 1917)
 In the mid-1950s, as ComPhibLant, was present for practice amphibious landings at Onslow Beach, North Carolina, 96-97

Federal Shipbuilding and Drydock Company, Kearny, New Jersey
 In the 1930s and 1940s built a number of destroyers for the U.S. Navy, 42, 55-56; special attention in 1944 went to the construction of the destroyer Ault (DD-698), 55

First Naval District
 Rear Admiral Leo H. Thebaud, who served 1949-52 as district commandant, was later invited back to the quarters for his 50th wedding anniversary, 10; Wylie resisted CNO Elmo Zumwalt's efforts to get him to retire in the early 1970s, 33, 35-36; during the Vietnam War period the staff lawyer and public affairs officer were useful in outlining tactics for dealing with anti-war demonstrators, 33-35

Fletcher, USS (DD-445)
 When the ship was commissioned in the summer of 1942, the crew contained three illiterates, 57-58; in the fall of 1942 had shakedown training and escorted convoys in the Caribbean, 56-57; during a November 1942 night surface action off Guadalcanal, Wylie made sketches of what he saw on the CIC radarscope, 37; in December 1942 recovered hundreds of men from the water after the sinking of the heavy cruiser Northampton (CA-26) off Guadalcanal, 51-52, 55-56

German Air Force
 Survivors of some aircraft downed in the Atlantic during World War II were executed if captured by Poles, 49

Germany
 In the early 1960s, as CinCNELM, Admiral H. P. Smith argued against Secretary of Defense Robert McNamara's planned removal of dependents from Germany, 97

Gloucester, Duke of
 A member of the British royal family, he was not properly polite in an exchange of radio messages in late 1934 with the Commander in Chief U.S. Asiatic Fleet, 30-31

Great Britain
 In the early 1960s Admiral Page Smith understood the role of supporting Great Britain and the Royal Navy, 78; in March 1967 the Liberian-flag tanker Torrey Canyon went aground off England and created a large oil spill, 79-80; in the mid-1960s a number of British citizens inquired about their country becoming part of the United States, 80-81

 See also: Naval Forces Europe, U.S.

Greece
　　In April 1967 a junta of Greek military officers seized control of the government, 71-74; U.S. plans for possible evacuation of King Constantine II, 73

Guadalcanal, Solomon Islands
　　On board the destroyer Fletcher (DD-445) during the November 1942 night surface action off Guadalcanal, Wylie made sketches of what he saw on the radarscope, 37; in December 1942 the Fletcher recovered hundreds of men from the water after the sinking of the heavy cruiser Northampton (CA-26) off Guadalcanal, 51-52, 55-56; in early 1943 the destroyer minesweeper Trever (DMS-16) delivered supplies to Marines on Guadalcanal, 29

Guns
　　Early in World War II the unreliable 1.1-inch antiaircraft guns on board U.S. Navy ships were replaced by 20-millimeter and 40-millimeter guns, 59

Hart, Rear Admiral Thomas C., USN (USNA, 1897)
　　In the early 1930s was rigorous but admired while serving as superintendent of the Naval Academy, 4-5

Hatch, Captain William M., USN
　　In 1967 was serving as intelligence officer for CinCUSNavEur when Greek military officers staged a coup, 71

Healy, Denis
　　Assessment of his performance in the mid-1960s as Britain's Minister of Defence, 79

Higgins, Rear Admiral John M., USN (USNA, 1922)
　　Near the end of World War II, as Commander Destroyer Squadron 62, used the Ault (DD-698) as his flagship, 54-55, 99; in the period shortly before the Korean War commanded Destroyer Flotilla One, 98-99; at the outset of the Korean War commanded Cruiser Division Five, 99

Holloway, Admiral James L., Jr., USN (USNA, 1919)
　　Went into Lebanon at the time of U.S. Marine landings in the summer of 1958 in his role as CinCNELM, 68-69

Holmes, Rear Admiral Ephraim P., USN (USNA, 1930)
　　In the mid-1950s was operations officer on the staff of Commander Amphibious Force Atlantic Fleet, 97, 102-103; in 1959, serving as Commander Cruiser Division Four, showed great forbearance while on board the USS Macon (CA-132), 103-104

Hong Kong
　　Became a thriving center for international affairs after the Communists took over mainland China in the late 1940s, 93

India
In the early 1960s, as CinCNELM, Admiral Page Smith was one of the few U.S. officials who could visit both India and Pakistan, 95

Ingersoll, Captain Royal E., USN (USNA, 1905)
In 1933 briefly commanded the heavy cruiser Augusta (CA-31) but chose not to take her to the Asiatic Fleet, 17-18

Intelligence
In 1933, two junior officers from the heavy cruiser Augusta (CA-31) encounter Communist recruiters in Seattle, a fact that naval intelligence promptly reported to their commanding officer, 19-20; interception in the spring of 1967 of indicators that Greek military officers were going to stage a coup, 71-72; in June 1967 Israeli forces attacked and badly damaged the U.S. intelligence ship Liberty (AGTR-5) near the Sinai peninsula, 74-77

Ireland
Early in World War II, the destroyer Bristol (DD-453) escorted convoys to from the United States to Londonderry, 48-49

Israel
In June 1967 Israeli forces attacked and badly damaged the U.S. intelligence ship Liberty (AGTR-5) near the Sinai Peninsula, 74-77

Italy
In the summer of 1929, during a training cruise, Naval Academy midshipmen gave a cheer for Pope Pius XI in the Vatican, 11-13; in the early 1960s a British naval officer from the SACLant staff visited Italy, 108-109

Joint Chiefs of Staff
Role in the autumn of 1956 during the Suez crisis, 66-67; role of during the Lebanon operation in 1958, 70; changes in the law in 1958 concerning the prerogatives of service chiefs, 84-85

Juneau, USS (CLAA-119)
At the outset of the Korean War in 1950 was the flagship for Rear Admiral John Higgins, Commander Cruiser Division Five, 99

Jurika, Captain Stephen, Jr., USN (USNA, 1933)
Served on the OpNav staff in the mid-1950s when plans for the Polaris ballistic missile submarine program were being formulated, 104-106

Kamikazes
In the summer of 1945, in Casco Bay, Maine, Vice Admiral Willis A. Lee, Jr., led an effort to find countermeasures against Japanese suicide planes, 23-24, 33

Kidd, Vice Admiral Isaac C., Jr., USN (USNA, 1942)
In 1967 did an excellent job of investigating the Israeli attack on the U.S. intelligence ship Liberty (AGTR-5), 76

Kotsch, Captain William J., USN
In the spring of 1967 provided predictions of oil movement after the Liberian-flag tanker Torrey Canyon grounded off the coast of England, 80

Lebanon
U.S. Marines landed in this nation in the summer of 1958 when civil war threatened, 68-70

Lee, Vice Admiral Willis A. Jr., USN (USNA, 1908)
In the summer of 1945, in Casco Bay, Maine, led an effort to find countermeasures against Japanese suicide planes, 23-24, 33

LeMay, General Curtis E., USAF
In the early 1950s, as head of the Strategic Air Command, was a guest speaker at the Naval War College, 89

Liberty, USS (AGTR-5)
Intelligence ship that in June 1967 was attacked and badly damaged by Israeli forces, 74-77

Long, Admiral Robert L. J., USN (USNA, 1944)
In the mid-1950s was involved in planning for the Polaris ballistic missile submarine program, 106-107

Long Beach, California
In March 1933 was hit by an earthquake, and the Navy provided relief measures, 21-22

Macon, USS (CA-132)
Heavy cruiser that in 1959 transited the newly opened St. Lawrence Seaway and visited Chicago, 103-104

Manila, Philippine Islands
In the mid-1930s the first Pan American clipper flying boat arrived in Manila, 93-94

Marine Corps, U.S.
In the early 1930s First Lieutenant Lewis Puller and his cohorts went to Nicaragua to chase rebel leader Augusto Sandino, 27-28; Marine detachment of the heavy cruiser Augusta (CA-31) during the early 1930s, 27-28, 31-32; in early 1943 the destroyer Trever (DMS-16) delivered supplies to Marines on Guadalcanal, 29; in the early 1950s the Naval War College did a study on the reasons for the existence of the Marine Corps, 89, 91-92; practice amphibious landings at Onslow Beach, North

Carolina, in the mid-1950s, 96-97; in the early 1970s Marine drug dealers were moved out of Portsmouth Naval Prison to keep them away from anti-Vietnam War demonstrators, 34-35; in the early 1970s anti-Vietnam War protesters chained themselves to the mast of the frigate Constitution in Boston, but Marines dealt with the situation in a way that minimized publicity, 34

Martin, Vice Admiral William I., USN (USNA, 1934)
Was Commander Sixth Fleet in the spring of 1967 when Greek military officers staged a coup, 72-73; role as fleet commander during the Six-Day War between Egypt and Israel in June 1967, 74-75, 78

Masterson, Vice Admiral Kleber S., USN (USNA, 1930)
In the spring of 1965, as Commander Second Fleet, went ashore with his flag lieutenant during the U.S. intervention in the Dominican Republic in response to a rebellion there, 64-65

McCain, Admiral John S., Jr., USN (Ret.) (USNA, 1931)
Served as Commander in Chief U.S. Naval Forces Europe during the June 1967 Six-Day War between Egypt and Israel, 75-76

McNamara, Robert S.
In the early 1960s, as CinCNELM, Admiral H. P. Smith argued against Secretary of Defense McNamara's planned removal of dependents from Germany, 97

Melbourne, Australia
In late 1934 the U.S. heavy cruiser Augusta (CA-31) paid a visit to this city, 30-32

Middle East Force, U.S.
Was beefed up with additional ships in June 1967, during the Six-Day War between Egypt and Israel, 74-75

Moffett, Captain William A., Jr., USN (USNA, 1930)
In the late 1940s was a student at the Naval War College, 86-87

Murfin, Admiral Orin G., USN (USNA, 1897)
In late 1935, while serving as Commander in Chief U.S. Asiatic Fleet, conducted diplomacy in Bangkok, Siam, 94-96

Mustin, Commander Lloyd M., USN (USNA, 1932)
While serving in the heavy cruiser Augusta (CA-31) in the early 1930s, argued that marksmanship required innate ability, 28; in 1945 was involved with Vice Admiral Willis Lee in seeking remedies against Japanese suicide aircraft, 23-24

Nautilus (Research Submarine)
In the summer of 1931 tried unsuccessfully to go under the arctic icecap and had to be towed to port by the battleship Wyoming (BB-32), 14

Naval Academy, Annapolis, Maryland
Course work in the late 1920s and early 1930s, 3, 6, 11; in the late 1920s the academy was looked down upon by students in civilian universities, 7-8; midshipman mischief, 4-5; summer training cruises in 1929 and 1931, 11-14; aviation indoctrination in 1930, 13; in the early 1930s Rear Admiral Thomas C. Hart was admired as superintendent, 4-5; hazing of underclassmen, 5-6; competition for class standing, 6-7; members of the class of 1932 who did well, 7; race-boat crews, 8-9; role of the executive department, 1939-41, 9-10, 40-41

Naval Forces Europe, U.S.
In the early 1960s Admiral Page Smith understood the role of supporting Great Britain and the Royal Navy, 78; support provided to the Royal Navy in the mid-1960s, 79-80; role of the command in the spring of 1967 during a military coup in Greece, 71-74; role of the command in June 1967 when Israeli forces attacked the intelligence ship Liberty (AGTR-5), 74-77; characteristics of Admiral John S. Thach as CinC in the mid-1960s, 77-79, 81-82

Naval Institute, U.S.
In the early 1950s officers at the Naval War College wrote articles for Proceedings magazine on naval strategy and explanations of the Navy's role, 89-92

Naval War College, Newport, Rhode Island
War gaming in the late 1940s, 86; studies in the early 1950s on the reasons for the existence of the Navy, 87-92; in the early 1950s Air Force officers were guest speakers at the college, 89; after completing the study on the Navy's role, war college officers wrote speeches and articles on the subject, 90-91

News Media
For the most part the media were positive in portraying the Navy in Boston in the early 1970s, during the Vietnam War, 34

New York City
In the mid-1950s received a visit from the amphibious warfare ships of Transport Division 24, 102-103

Nicaragua
In the early 1930s First Lieutenant Lewis Puller and other Marines went to Nicaragua to chase rebel leader Augusto Sandino, 28

Nimitz, Fleet Admiral Chester W., USN (USNA, 1905)
In the mid-1930s commanded the heavy cruiser Augusta (CA-31) on the U.S. West Coast and in the Asiatic Fleet, 17-20, 25-26, 32; qualities of while commanding the Pacific Fleet during World War II, 18-19

Nixon, Vice President Richard M.
In May 1958, when Nixon was in Venezuela, the U.S. Navy had an aircraft carrier stationed offshore for a possible rescue of the Vice President, 61

Northampton, USS (CA-26)
In December 1942 the destroyer Fletcher (DD-445) recovered hundreds of men from the water after the sinking of the Northampton off Guadalcanal, 51-52, 55-56

North Atlantic Treaty Organization (NATO)
As Commander Amphibious Group Two in the early 1950s, Rear Admiral Harold Page Smith gave a speech on amphibious warfare to the NATO Defense College, 90; in the early 1960s, as CinCNELM, Admiral Smith argued against Secretary of Defense Robert McNamara's planned removal of dependents from Germany, 97; in the early 1960s a British naval officer from the SACLant staff visited Italy and Portugal, 108-109; Wylie's recommendation to revise the NATO treaty, 109

Oklahoma City, USS (CLG-5)
In the early 1960s, as flagship for Commander Cruiser-Destroyer Flotilla Nine, was viewed by Wylie as being top-heavy, 110

Pakistan
In the early 1960s, as CinCNELM, Admiral Page Smith was one of the few U.S. officials who could visit both India and Pakistan, 95

Pan American World Airways
In the mid-1930s the first clipper flying boat arrived in the Manila, Philippine Islands, 93-94

Philippine Islands
In the mid-1930s the first Pan American clipper flying boat arrived in Manila, 93-94

Pius XI, Pope
In the summer of 1929, during a training cruise, Naval Academy midshipmen gave a cheer for the Pope in the Vatican, 11-13

Polaris Program
Role of the OpNav staff in the mid-1950s as plans for the ballistic missile submarine program were being formulated, 104-107

Polish Navy
Operated with the Allies in World War II because of great bitterness toward Germany, 49

Portsmouth (New Hampshire) Naval Prison
In the early 1970s Marine drug dealers were moved out of the prison to keep them away from anti-Vietnam War demonstrators, 34-35

Portugal
In the early 1960s a British naval officer from the SACLant staff visited Portugal on NATO business, 108-109

Promotion of Officers
Until 1960 no U.S. naval officer from the SACLant staff had been selected for flag rank, 107-108

Providence, USS (CLG-6)
In the early 1960s, as flagship for Commander Cruiser-Destroyer Flotilla Nine, was viewed by Wylie as being top-heavy, 110

Puller, Lieutenant Colonel Lewis B., USMC
In the early 1930s Puller and other Marines went to Nicaragua to chase rebel leader Augusto Sandino, 28; in the mid-1930s he served in the Marine detachment of the heavy cruiser Augusta (CA-31), 27-28, 31-32; in early 1943 he and Wylie had a drink together when they met on Guadalcanal, 29

Radar
In 1943, under the leadership of Rear Admiral Mahlon Tisdale, the Destroyer Force Pacific Fleet worked on developing shipboard combat information center doctrine, 36-40; in 1945, Task Force 69 in Casco Bay, Maine, tested radar with a moving target indicator as a possible remedy against Japanese suicide planes, 23-24

Reid, USS (DD-369)
Destroyer that went into commission in 1936 under the command of Commander Robert B. Carney and made a shakedown cruise to the Mediterranean, 42-43; as a "gold-plater," the ship was much more modern than the four-stackers of the World War I era, 44

Religion
In the summer of 1929, during a training cruise, Naval Academy midshipmen gave a cheer for Pope Pius XI in the Vatican, 11-13

Replenishment at Sea
As done in the 1960-61 period by ships of Cruiser-Destroyer Flotilla Nine, 92-93

Rescue at Sea
In December 1942 the destroyer Fletcher (DD-445) recovered hundreds of men from the water after the sinking of the heavy cruiser Northampton (CA-26) off Guadalcanal, 51-52, 55-56; in 1944-45 the destroyer Ault (DD-698) rescued dozens of downed naval aviators, 52-55

Research, Office of Naval
   In the years right after World War II Wylie was involved in human engineering research, 85-86

Richardson, Captain James O., USN (USNA, 1902)
   Avuncular officer who commanded the heavy cruiser Augusta (CA-31) in the early 1930s, 17-28

Robards, Ensign William C. F., USN (USNA, 1932)
   In the early 1930s, while serving in the heavy cruiser Augusta (CA-31), had an encounter with Communists in Seattle, 19-20

Roe, Colonel Thomas George Roe, USMC
   In the early 1950s, while at the Naval War College, did a study on the reasons for the existence of the Marine Corps, 89, 91-92

Royal Navy
   In late 1934 a British cruiser, with the Duke of Gloucester on board, visited Melbourne, Australia, 30-31; in the early 1960s, as CinCNELM, Admiral Page Smith understood the role of supporting Great Britain and the Royal Navy, 78; in the early 1960s a British naval officer from the SACLant staff visited Italy, 108-109; support provided in the mid-1960s by U.S. Naval Forces Europe, 79-80

Sabin, Vice Admiral Lorenzo S., Jr., USN (USNA, 1921)
   In the early 1960s served as Deputy CinCLant and helped Wylie get selected for flag rank, 107-108

SACLant (Supreme Allied Commander Atlantic)
   Until 1960 no U.S. naval officer from the SACLant staff had been selected for flag rank, 107-108

St. Lawrence Seaway
   In 1959 the heavy cruiser Macon (CA-132) transited the newly opened seaway and visited Chicago, 103-104

Saint-Pierre and Miquelon
   In the early part of World War II the governor and his wife were captured by the Free French, 48-49

San Pedro, California
   In March 1933 was hit by an earthquake, and the Navy provided relief measures, 21-22

Second Fleet, U.S.
   In the spring of 1965 provided ships and men in response to a rebellion in the Dominican Republic, 61-65

Selection Boards
Until 1960 no U.S. naval officer from the SACLant staff had been selected for flag rank, 107-108

Shanghai, China
In the mid-1930s, the heavy cruiser Augusta (CA-31), flagship of the U.S. Asiatic Fleet, visited this port often, 16, 24-25

Shear, Commander Harold E., USN (USNA, 1942)
Served on the OpNav staff in the mid-1950s when plans for the Polaris ballistic missile submarine program were being formulated, 105-107

Siam
In late 1935, as Commander in Chief U. S. Asiatic Fleet, Admiral Orin G. Murfin performed diplomatic service in Bangkok, 94-96

Sixth Fleet, U.S.
Responded with ships on station in reaction to the Suez crisis of 1956 and the Lebanon crisis of 1958, 65-70; in the spring of 1967 moved toward Greece at the time of a military coup there, 72-74; in June 1967 Israeli forces attacked and badly damaged the U.S. intelligence ship Liberty (AGTR-5) near the Sinai peninsula, 74-77

Smith, Admiral Harold Page, USN (USNA, 1924)
As Commander Amphibious Group Two in the early 1950s, gave a speech on amphibious warfare to the NATO Defense College, 90; as ComPhibGru 2, fired a ship's commanding officer whom he considered unsatisfactory, 96-97; in the early 1960s, as CinCNELM, understood the role of supporting Great Britain and the Royal Navy, 78; as CinCNELM visited India and Pakistan, 95; discussion with Secretary of Defense Robert McNamara about removal of dependents from Germany, 97; role as Commander in Chief Atlantic Fleet in the spring of 1965, when the Navy had ships stationed off the Dominican Republic during a time of unrest and eventually sent Marines into the country to maintain order, 61-65; personal characteristics, 97-98

Speck, Captain Robert H., USN (USNA, 1927)
In the mid-1950s was chief of staff for Commander Amphibious Force Atlantic Fleet, 97; in 1953-54 commanded Transport Division 24 in the Atlantic Fleet, 102-103

Spock, Dr. Benjamin
Noted pediatrician who led antiwar protests in the late 1960s and early 1970s, 33-35

Submarines
Role of the OpNav staff in the mid-1950s as plans for the Polaris ballistic missile submarine program were being formulated, 104-107

Suez Canal
    Response of the U.S. Navy in the fall of 1956 after President Gamal Nasser nationalized the canal and U.S. allies sent military forces to the area, 65-68

Thach, Admiral John S., USN (USNA, 1927)
    In the mid-1960s served as Commander in Chief U.S. Naval Forces Europe, 71, 77-79, 81-82; personal characteristics, 77-79

Thailand
    See: Siam

Thebaud, Commander Leo H., USN (USNA, 1913)
    In the early 1940s served as executive officer for the commandant of midshipmen at the Naval Academy, 9-10; personal characteristics, 10; served 1949-52 as commandant of the First Naval District, 10

Tisdale, Rear Admiral Mahlon S., USN (USNA, 1912)
    In the early 1940s served as commandant of midshipmen at the Naval Academy, 9; in 1943, under Tisdale's leadership, the Pacific Fleet Destroyer Force worked on developing shipboard combat information center doctrine, 36-40; arranged in January 1944 for Wylie to be transferred to the West Coast and a new ship, 38-39

Torpedoes
    During the early part of World War II U.S. Navy torpedoes were notoriously unreliable, 58-60

Torrey Canyon (Liberian-flag Tanker)
    In March 1967 went aground off England and created a large oil spill, 79-80

Trever, USS (DMS-16)
    In early 1943 this destroyer minesweeper delivered supplies to Marines on the island of Guadalcanal, 29; Wylie had a short command tour, 36-37; dirty, run-down condition of the ship in World War II, 44; pilfering of beer by a crew member was handled by an unofficial disciplinary system, 44-45

Trinidad
    In the fall of 1942 the destroyer Fletcher (DD-445) escorted convoys in the vicinity of Trinidad, 56-57

Tyree, Rear Admiral David M., USN (USNA, 1925)
    From 1959 to 1963 served as Commandeer Naval Support Force Antarctica, 111

Uniform Code of Military Justice
    Differences in application from the pre-World War II Articles for the Government of the Navy, 24-26; use of during Vietnam War protests, 34-35

Upham, Admiral Frank B., USN (USNA, 1893)
　　In late 1934, as Commander in Chief U.S. Asiatic Fleet, rode the heavy cruiser Augusta (CA-31) to Australia for a visit, 30

Venezuela
　　In May 1958 the U.S. Navy had an aircraft carrier stationed offshore during unrest in the country for a possible rescue of Vice President Richard Nixon, 61

Vietnam War
　　In the mid-1960s the OpNav section dealing with riverine warfare received a copy of a 1950s Naval War College study on shoal and inland waters, 92; during the 1969-72 period the First Naval District staff lawyer and public affairs officer were useful in outlining tactics for dealing with anti-war demonstrators, 33-35

White, General Thomas D., USAF (USMA, 1920)
　　In the early 1950s, as Vice Chief of Staff of the Air Force, was a guest speaker at the Naval War College, 89

Whiting, Commander Francis E. M., USN (USNA, 1912)
　　In 1934 was executive officer of the heavy cruiser Augusta (CA-31) when the ship visited Australia and the Philippines, 31-32

Wylie, Rear Admiral Joseph C., Jr., USN (Ret.) (USNA, 1932)
　　Parents of, 1-3; boyhood in the 1910s and 1920s in New Jersey, 1-3, 15; education of, 3, 6, 15; wife of, 1, 41-42; children of, 1, 16; preparation in the late 1920s to enter the Naval Academy, 1-3; from 1928 to 1932 was a Naval Academy midshipman, 3-9, 11-15; in 1932-36 was a junior officer in the heavy cruiser Augusta (CA-31), 15-22, 24-28, 30; from 1936 to 1938 was in the original crew of the destroyer Reid (DD-369), 42-43; in 1938-39 served in the destroyer tender Altair (AD-11), 46-47; from 1939 to 1941 served in the Naval Academy's executive department, 9-10, 40-41; in 1941-42 was executive officer of the new destroyer Bristol (DD-453), 47-50; in 1942 was executive officer in the original crew of the destroyer Fletcher (DD-445), 37, 51-52; in early 1943 commanded the destroyer minesweeper Trever (DMS-16), 29, 36-37, 44-45; during the latter part of 1943 worked on the staff of Commander Destroyer Force Pacific Fleet, 36-40; in 1944-45 commanded the destroyer Ault (DD-698), 18-19, 52-53; in 1945-48 worked with the Office of Naval Research, 85-86; in 1948-49 was a student at the Naval War College, 86-87; in 1949-50 was operations officer on the staff of Commander Destroyer Flotilla One, 92-93; in 1950-53 was assigned to the Naval War College, 87-92; in 1953-54 commanded the attack cargo ship Arneb (AKA-56), 100-103; in 1954-55 was on the staff of Commander Amphibious Group Two, 90, 96-97; served 1955-58 on the OpNav staff in Washington, 65-70, 104-107; in 1958-59 commanded the heavy cruiser Macon (CA-132), 103-104; served 1959-60 on the staff of the Supreme Allied Commander Atlantic, 107-110; in 1960-61 was Commander Cruiser-Destroyer Flotilla Nine, 92-93, 110; in 1961-62 was the Navy's Deputy Inspector

General, 111-114; in 1964-66 served on the staff of Commander in Chief Atlantic Fleet, 61-65, 108; in 1966-67 was Deputy Commander in Chief U.S. Naval Forces Europe, 71-75; from 1969 to 1972 served twilight tour as commandant of the First Naval District, 10, 33-36

Wyoming, USS (BB-32)
In June 1931, during a midshipman training cruise, had to rescue the research submarine Nautilus after her unsuccessful attempt to go under the arctic icecap, 14

Zumwalt, Admiral Elmo R., Jr., USN (USNA, 1943)
As Chief of Naval Operations in the early 1970s, issued Z-grams that affected many enlisted personnel, 26; as CNO got rid of talented officers to bring in younger replacements, 33-36; tried to get Wylie to retire, 35-36

www.ingramcontent.com/pod-product-compliance
Lightning Source LLC
Chambersburg PA
CBHW082208070526

44585CB00020B/2336